EVERY
STEP COUNTS

Your Guide to the Challenging Path
of Marketing a Book

DAVID LOY AND **CHASE NEELY**

Every Step Counts

© 2022 by David Loy and Chase Neely.

eBook ISBN: 978-1-73558-729-5

To you, Reader,
May your book reach its full potential and
your message reach as many people as possible

ACKNOWLEDGMENTS

The first core value of Leverage is Faith and Family First. The work our company does is important and it must be done at a high level in order for the business to be successful, but nothing we do at Leverage is as important as our personal faith in Jesus Christ. That faith will always be our first acknowledgement.

Beyond our shared faith, we are both eager to thank our wives. Being married to us can't be easy but both Joy (Chase) and Stephanie (David) consistently show patience and provide support for what we do. They deserve far more than we can offer in a short paragraph.

The individuals who comprise the team at Leverage are the primary reason this book was written. Our company exists because of the people who show up with us each day. They keep us sharp, they challenge our thinking, and they produce outstanding work. We are proud to know each one of them as people and as co-workers.

Lastly, we want to draw special attention to Jerry Jenkins. In addition to being the preeminent online teacher of writing, he's one of the most prolific authors of all time. But Jerry's skill set and resume are nothing compared to the person he is behind the scenes. He works diligently, with humility, passion, and a daily desire to obey the calling God has placed on his life. He has been the perfect cornerstone client for Leverage and he's been both a friend and mentor to us for years. Jerry and Dianna: You are loved and appreciated greatly.

TABLE OF CONTENTS

INTRODUCTION

From Chase:

Recently, David and I were looking on the internet for a book for authors about how to best build their platform and market their book.

Because of our experience in the area, we were pretty picky as to what would and wouldn't work for us. Eventually, we came to the realization that if we wanted a book that matched the advice that we've given to dozens of authors over the course of the last decade, we would need to write it ourselves.

So, we did.

What follows is our best advice for you.

Because, we want you to succeed. We want your message to reach as many people as possible online and in print.

So, over the course of the next 25 chapters, we are going to lay out everything we've learned.

We've had a lot of successes, but we've also had a great deal of failures.

Learn from us so that you can make the most of your message.

People need to hear it!

From David:

Writing a book is hard work. I've seen that fact play out in hundreds of authors over the course of my career, and I've experienced it myself in the writing of this book. It's hard, but it's not impossible. Marketing a book is also hard. It is also not impossible.

Authors often struggle to switch out of the mindset of writing a great manuscript into the mindset of marketing that manuscript. If you haven't done so yet, think about the difference in mindset between writing a book and marketing the book. They are completely different tasks and they require several different skills to execute well. It's a tough transition for anyone, and even when you are able to make that mindset jump, you are met with more options than the menu at The Cheesecake Factory. There are so many things you could be doing, and so many differing opinions to consider. The amount of choices you face are overwhelming at times.

The chapters that follow have been written with the hope of helping you to navigate those choices efficiently. We believe these ideas will expedite your learning curve.

This book is not a magic formula. It won't make your book marketing efforts easy, but it will help you to move more quickly and more confidently as you impact others with your writing.

PART I

Building a Platform

How can you have a chicken without an egg?

"Platform" is becoming one of the most irritating words throughout the entertainment industry, because the onus to building a fanbase is shifting from the companies (who used to do it as a core competency) to the talent (who needed the companies to do it in the first place).

This is bringing about a new generation of talented individuals who are rockstar creatives and talented marketers, which leads to whole new questions about the purpose of companies that exploit the copyrights of the talent.

You might be feeling this tension as an author, and it's the reason why we start the book here. Author marketing has become nearly synonymous with building a platform, and yet, there's very little practical advice on how to do it.

Publishing companies were left in the digital dust when it came to building platforms online (though they're starting to catch up) and authors were forced to figure it out on their own.

In this section, we answer crucial platform-related questions, so that you can clear the mental space to start writing an amazing book.

Let's be honest: The world loses when its authors are more focused on social media marketing than they are on transformational content. We've built this handy how-to guide to clear the confusion and bring you into the digital age with a thunderclap—so that you amplify your message with maximum impact and minimum mistakes. We're excited to continue with you on this journey, as it's one we've made with dozens of authors looking to make the transition from talented writer to author who writes for their career.

One note before we get started though: This is a book about author marketing — it's not about the writing process. You have to have that part squared away before any of this matters. You can be an amazing marketer and a terrible writer (present company included), so you need to make sure that the work (meaning, the actual writing) is amazing. That's the bar. That's the bare minimum. That's what agents and publishers expect: Amazing writing with a platform.

You can't have the chicken without the egg.

With that note, let's begin with one of the questions we get asked most frequently:

CHAPTER 1:

What Is a Platform and Why Do You Need One?

"Platform" has become one of the most commonly used words in recent years, but many people still don't understand what it actually means.

The term used to only refer to a stage or raised surface which would make speakers or performers easier to see by an audience.

Then a new meaning became attached—one that refers to a political program, policy, or group. (Don't worry, that last sentence is as far as we will get into anything related to politics in this book!)

And out of those two previous definitions for the word, the term "platform" was adopted by the internet-age of authors, speakers, and message bearers to encompass a person's collective strategy for influencing other people in their target audience.

The turning point seems to be around the time that Michael Hyatt released his seminal book on the topic in 2012: *Platform: Get Noticed in a Noisy World.*

Michael Hyatt was one of the first to use his previous successes (as a CEO of one of the major publishing companies) to build an online platform. The path he lays out to that success in his book put words to the tension that authors were feeling. The publishing companies of the twenty-first century were more interested in publishing books of authors with successful online platforms than creating platforms for talented writers who were as of yet undiscovered.

Their decision in that regard was neither right or wrong—it just became the truth of the moment. Any author looking to be traditionally published needed to know how to build an online platform on their own. (No help for self-published authors either, by the way—the nature of self-publishing means you are building the platform by yourself.) But what does it mean to build a platform?

"Platform" as it relates to you as an author means anything you are doing to create, sustain, or grow the potential number of people who will read your book.

- Do you have a website where you write blog posts?

- Do you contribute articles to a publication?

- Are you active on any social media pages?

- Do you have an email list of people to which you regularly send messages with an intention to deliver value?

- Do you lead a company or department?

- Do you host a small group or teach a class?

- Do you pastor a church?

- Does your work allow you consistent opportunities to meet with new people or to present in front of groups of people?

- Do you give motivational or educational speeches?

- Do you host a podcast?

- Do you have a YouTube channel?

- Do you engage in internet communities?

These are just a few common examples, but a "yes" to any of these questions means you already have a platform, or at least the start of one.

Are you being intentional about how you engage your platform? Do you know how to grow it?

The answer to these questions is likely why you're here, and we will certainly dive into engaging and growing a platform. But before we do, let's ask an even more basic question:

Why is a platform necessary?

Going back to the original meaning of the word "platform," it was necessary to raise a surface so that the performer could be seen by everyone in the audience.

In the same way, the reason an online platform is necessary is so your message can be seen. So it can be heard. So it can be viewed, reviewed, shared, discussed, commented on, supported, argued with, and challenged ... all of this happening whether you are actively engaged in those exchanges or not.

And in all honesty, the platform building that used to work for publishing houses—book tours, book stores, signings, PR, and sales channels—proved unpredictable and thus, resulted in a failure rate of nearly 70 percent. So, in an effort to increase the certainty, they were placing bets on sure things. Audiences that already had been developed in niches that were already proven by authors who had already put in the work. So, to even be *noticed* by publishing companies, the platform is a necessity.

Think about it for a moment from their point of view: Maybe you've written a wonderful book that could be enjoyed by millions, but if no one else knows you are an author, your book will never be read by anyone else. Who's going to pay for that development? And even if someone is willing to take the financial risk, who is going to take the time and devote the staffing it will require in order to make it worth their while?

The publishing companies can't afford to, and it's not in their core competency. (Believe me: We took over the website for Jerry Jenkins from a publishing house, and yowza! Not good. Of course they were well-intentioned and tried their best to create a useful website for Jerry, but it was not using the best practices from what we know about digital marketing. And it looked bad. Take a trip on the internet archive's wayback machine and type in "jerryjenkins.com" in the search bar. You won't be disappointed.)

Plus, you don't want them to pay for the development. Because, again, it's not in their core competency. They are not there to create your platform. They are there to print, publish, and distribute your book. They can enhance an existing platform and they can help it to achieve accelerated growth, but their business model is not focused on helping authors build a platform from scratch.

It's better for you to make the effort to create the platform. It is not quicker or easier, but it is better. Doing so will also allow you to gain tremendous amounts of knowledge about your customers and how you should go about maintaining and growing that platform in the future.

Why? Because having and building your platform will maximize your impact—and that goes way beyond the message of one book. A sustainable platform gives you the ability to create a career as an author.

That leads us to another question we get asked all the time:

Does every author need a platform?

Our answer: No. Only those authors who want readers need a platform. :-) If you are writing a book strictly for your own private use or for your family to read, you don't need a platform. But if you want your book to reach beyond your household, then yes—we believe you need a platform.

CHAPTER 2:

How to Define Your Target Audience

We briefly mentioned above that a core component to a platform is the ability to reach your target audience. Having a target audience is essential for authors, both as you write and as you plan out your marketing strategy.

A common mistake is for an author to say, "My book is for everyone."

It's great to have that much confidence in your book, but that statement is not going to help you in attracting people to your work.

Trust us, we've seen authors make this mistake, and it's cost them a lot of opportunities. One author in particular was a rockstar in the education niche, but wanted to expand. We pushed him to remain focused in the space and while he was, he continued to achieve incredible results. The organic search results skyrocketed for his website content. New people in his niche were seeing his name and his material regularly. His email list grew by the thousands. Things were going exactly as we'd planned and agreed upon. And then, he couldn't wait to expand into other niches with different target audiences.

We call it the Squirrel Syndrome—if you've ever seen the movie *Up!* from Pixar, you may remember Doug, the dog who can talk and follows the main characters around. When he starts telling them crucial information, he often gets distracted by the squirrels that cross his path, exclaiming, "Squirrel!" Authors who pursue every opportunity instead of staying focused on their most appropriate niche are like Doug. They wander around and chase every squirrel, forsaking the opportunity at hand.

Don't be a Doug. Don't fall victim to Squirrel Syndrome.

It's simply not necessary to think this way. You've written a book with a core message that will impact a particular person more than another. By focusing on that target, your book will organically reach more people both inside and outside of the target market.

Think of who would benefit the most from reading your book.

It might start with those who love the genre you are writing in ... but who is that person?

How old are they?

- What other books are they likely to have read if they are reading yours?

- What are a few life experiences they are likely to have gone through?

- What is their biggest pain point?

If you struggle to get started on defining your target audience, start with yourself. You might be a great example of the target audience you are trying to reach. If you're not in your target audience, you can try two tools we've put together below.

The first is a brand strategy template. The second is an empathy map.

Brand Strategy Template

<u>What is a Brand Strategy?</u>

For our purposes today, we'll define brand strategy as:

The steps your business must take to get from "I have an idea" to "I'm making money."

In this brand strategy template, we'll address the three major components of a failsafe brand strategy:

1. A clear Purpose Statement

2. A narrowly defined Target Audience

3. Consistent Brand Messaging

How to Create a Brand Strategy

Using the three components to brand strategy above, let's break down the process of creating your brand strategy step-by-step, so you have everything you need to get started.

1. Identify Your Brand's Purpose

Your goal in this step is to find the answer to a single question:

Why is my brand in business?

Full disclosure:

Your answer can be altruistic or selfish (we recommend altruism), but the main thing is that it must be sincere.

As an example of a "me-focused" purpose statement, look at Richard Branson:

"To have fun in [my] journey through life and learn from [my] mistakes."

If you go the altruistic route, the format you're looking for is:

"I help X person accomplish Y goal."

At Leverage, ours is:

"We exist to give renowned thought leaders the ability to reach as many people as they can with their message online."

Then, you want to boil that down into a mantra that you can easily use in internal and external communications. Bonus points if you can narrow it down to one word.

Ours is simply:

Amplify.

So, how do you determine your brand's purpose statement?

First—

Identify your core values.

Your core values determine how you will live out your purpose statement and the types of people who will be in your audience.

Let's look at Oprah Winfrey for an example.

We can't know her core values without getting some inside info, but we can guess from her purpose statement:

"To be a teacher. And to be known for inspiring my students to be more than they thought they could be."

that she values…

Continuous learning…

Encouragement…

Inspiration…

…with the ultimate goal that, by living out those values, she will lead her students to action.

How did we come up with those values?

We looked at her purpose statement.

Notice the teacher/student language she uses and the inspiration language tied to helping her students take action.

As you can see, your values tie directly into your purpose statement.

And the second major factor in your purpose statement is your audience.

Defining your core values will make your mission statement more genuine, which should make it resonate more with that audience.

An insincere attempt to resonate with an audience that doesn't align with your core purpose isn't going to flatter anyone.

In Step 2, we'll show you how to gain a better understanding of your target audience.

2. Identify Your Target Audience

We almost used Coca Cola as a brand strategy example earlier in this post. But we left them out for a very specific reason—

They have the broadest target audience we've ever seen in a mission statement (emphasis is ours):

"To refresh *the world*…To inspire moments of optimism and happiness…To create value and make a difference."

Check that out.

"To refresh the WORLD!"

That broad of a target audience works for a global brand. But it's a bad example for right now.

Why?

Great brand strategies for young businesses focus on a narrowly defined audience.

Conquer that niche first. Then, in 100 years, you too can use the entire world as your audience!

For now, think about who your core offering would help the most.

Be specific.

Your goal is to create an "avatar" — a detailed representation of your one best customer.

If you're in the real estate business, your avatar might be Jim, a 32-year-old computer programmer with a wife and two young sons who needs to buy a house so he can start his new job.

Ideally, you would know as much information as possible about Jim— things like his biggest challenge with buying a house, his hobbies, the shows he likes to watch, his favorite books, even some of his favorite foods.

If that sounds creepy, remember two things:

Jim is not a real person. He's just a representation of your target market. He's not going to get creeped out, we promise.

The purpose of creating an avatar is to serve your customers better. If you know what they're like, you're better equipped to give them what they need.

The better you understand your avatar, the more likely you are to connect with them in your brand messaging too. The empathy map example a little later on will help you with this process as well.

Finally, to round out your brand strategy, you need to move to step 3.

3. Communicate Your Brand's Purpose to Your Target Audience

We can talk about branding fails ad infinitem.

Pepsi's failed Kendall Jenner commercial...

Zaxby's "Open on Sundays" commercial…

Lifelock CEO's dare to steal his identity…

…and these are just off the top of our heads.

So, how do you avoid ending up on a list like this?

Always tie your brand's messaging to its core purpose.

Every branding decision you make — from website copy to brand colors to logo — should reflect your brand's core promise to its target customers.

The most successful brands do this over and over again.

Toyota: The Brand Messaging Consistency Test

Let's take a peek under the hood of Toyota's brand messaging (Not even sorry for that pun.):

Does their brand messaging consistently communicate their purpose to their target audience?

Their stated purpose:

"To attract and attain customers with high-valued products and services and the most satisfying ownership experience in America."

Round 1: Internal Messaging

The Toyota Way is a guiding principle that Toyota uses for internal operations. Let's see where that fits in here.

Here's a blurb on the Toyota Way from their European Website (emphasis ours):

"The Toyota Way is built on two pillars: **Continuous Improvement**, which takes in the concepts of Challenge, Kaizen and Genchi Genbutsu, and **Respect for People**, which embraces Respect and Teamwork."

Does that align with their stated purpose?

"Continuous Improvement" certainly seems like a way to guarantee that services and products remain of high value…

That one passes the test.

But what about "Respect for People?"

Will that guarantee "the most satisfying ownership experience?"

Imagine your Corolla is out of alignment, so you take it to a Toyota dealership.

The whole time you're there, you're treated with respect and your car gets the repair it needs. You might even get some free coffee or a snack while you wait.

Sounds satisfying to us!

All right, so this internal culture built around continuous improvement and respect for people *does* line up directly with their purpose statement.

Fine, Toyota. You win that one…

Round 2: External Messaging

Let's keep this simple.

When we do a Google search of "Toyota ads," each ad speaks to why you should love owning one of these cars.

Whether it's the truck taking you off-road, the hybrid protecting the environment, or the concept car keeping you at the cutting edge of innovation, the message is clear:

Owning a Toyota is satisfying.

You should also notice that these Toyotas look extremely high value.

Of course, that's nothing new to car ads, but they back up these pictures with social proof of awards that prove the high value.

They hit the nail on the head. Again.

Results?

Toyota gets it.

Here's how you can be like them:

Let your purpose flow through your company's culture and the communication between your staff.

Let that internal communication and commitment to the brand's purpose flow outwardly in your marketing material.

Don't forsake any step along the way. It's hard work. It's necessary work.

Now that we've walked through how to craft your brand strategy. Let's dive a little bit deeper into how your brand can fully understand your target audience using an empathy map.

Empathy Map

Dave Gray first developed the empathy map as a tool to understand users in a development setting. (Think user interface software development.)

That includes what they…

Think

See

Hear

Say

Do

…while using your product.

By thinking through and visually exploring these things, you are able to develop a customized experience for them.

We use an empathy map to understand our customers on a deeper level, but instead of analyzing how they interact with our product…

We look at how they interact with the outside world.

If that sounds vague, think of the empathy map as a way to walk a mile in your customer's shoes.

Quick note: All the advice in this section assumes you have correctly identified your target audience in the brand strategy section above.

When you create an empathy map for marketing purposes, you think through what your target customer…

Thinks

Sees

Hears

Says

Does

…in his/her daily life.

As a result, you develop empathy for that person. (Duh!)

All that information gives you insight into what your target customer feels.

This is the beauty of the map.

By going through the exercise, you can start to identify the things that are holding your customer back—their biggest pains.

Then, you can transform those pains into the biggest wins your customer can experience—their biggest potential gains.

It's almost like you're able to wave a magic wand to fix the biggest problem your customer is experiencing.

Your book can speak directly to that problem and provide the clearest way to overcome it!

This is extremely powerful. In fact, it's the essence of effective marketing.

We believe building an empathy map is an absolute necessity if you want to get into the mind of your target audience, which is extremely helpful when you're launching a book and building your platform.

It's crucial for both marketing copy and user experience.

And what's more: It helps you home in on exactly who you are trying to reach as you're building your platform.

CHAPTER 3:

Competitor Research and Review Mining

Bestselling author and writing coach Jerry Jenkins often says, "Good authors are good readers, great authors are great readers."

If this is true, are you a great author? Are you a good author?

That statement bothers some because they want to avoid being compared to other authors ... or maybe because they don't want to take on the daunting task of reading that many books!

But if you pause to think through the concept, you'll likely agree with the statement. And not only is it a helpful concept to keep in mind as you learn the craft of writing, but it will also be tremendously helpful for gathering a baseline of books to use in competitive research.

Imagine having read 100 books in your genre. If you haven't done this yet, start now.

If you have read 100 books in your genre, then of course you have been immersed in the work of those who are successful at what you are wanting to do. But you are also stocking up on the ammo you'll need when it comes time to pitch and promote your work. It is much easier to talk about the value your book brings when you are well-educated on what others in your genre are doing.

Having comparisons and contrasts at the ready is going to be essential as you tell others why your book matters. Remember, your book matters only to you until you figure out a way to communicate to others why it should matter to them. Don't assume anyone will automatically care as much about your book as you do. Instead, start thinking about what value other people are doing to receive from reading your book. Why should someone devote their time to reading what you've written? What is the takeaway for the reader? These questions are easier to answer the more you've read and studied other authors in your genre.

In addition to reading other books from your genre, another productive exercise is to read *reviews* of other books from your genre.

This is especially helpful while you are still in the writing and editing stage but it can also be useful for marketing purposes.

You need to know what the public thinks about your genre. What do they like? What is commonly mentioned in reviews as being something readers love?

What cautionary comments found in reviews of other books should you consider applying to your work?

It's a given that reading internet reviews can be problematic. A high level of discernment must be applied but when done well, the mining of reviews can be a great way to spend time in preparing your marketing materials and even in the honing of your manuscript itself. Not every online review is useful, but neither is every online review useless. Take the time to sift through reviews and find common themes. Make note of what you learn and then be intentional about how you integrate that information into both your writing and your marketing efforts.

We've heard from several authors (most often in nonfiction) that going through online reviews can lead to an author questioning their idea. Seeing so many books that are already written about your topic, and seeing so many reviews about those books have a tendency to cause authors to shut down creatively. Be prepared to fight those thoughts and feelings if you find yourself in that situation. Here's how:

The most important thing to consider while you are mining for reviews and doing competitor research is: You are bringing YOU to your book.

Read those words again. <u>You are bringing you to your book.</u>

If you've lost track of that fact, write it down and place it where you can see it every day. Use information from others around you, but don't forget that you have a unique take to offer.

If the saying "nothing is new under the sun" is true, then the story or concepts you are writing about aren't new. And that is fine. The sooner you accept that what you are writing about isn't "new," the better. No one is expecting you to write about something completely new. The "new" comes from you.

If you write authentically and with purpose, you don't need to worry about your book being unique. Your perspective, your writing voice, your creativity and experiences … That is what matters. That's the "new " part of your book.

For a deeper dive into the review mining process and into competitor research, see Part IV of this book.

CHAPTER 4:

Consistency across Outlets

Can you recall a recent time when you were confused about what someone was offering? Maybe it was a commercial you saw or an ad on YouTube. Or maybe it was a sales pitch you heard from a local insurance provider. If you are struggling to remember the last time you were confused, that's OK too, and it goes to prove our point.

How do you feel when you are confused?

Sometimes people seek clarification on their own when they are confused. Other times, people will pause and think through the confusing situation and try to problem solve on their own. But in the majority of cases when confusion strikes, people have too many other things going on around them, or they just don't want to pause and try to understand what is being communicated. Instead of figuring out what it is they could or should do, they simply move on.

If you couldn't think of an example of the last time you were confused, you are proof that people usually just move on. They stop the confusion by leaving the situation, clicking away from ads, or by changing the channel.

Dr. Les Parrot is a former client of our company and he's been a kind friend in the years since. He is known for many sayings and ideas around love, communication, and marriages, but one of the concepts he teaches that is most widely applicable (and has stuck with us for a long time) is: *Clarify the Content*.

Dr. Parrot says this specifically in the context of communication in a relationship and how essential it is for both parties to be clear on what the other is saying.

The concept of *Clarify the Content* is equally important when you are building a platform.

If you as the "brand" are not clear on who you are and what you are offering, the consumer will not be clear either. In fact, they will be the opposite of clear. They will be confused.

Confused people don't convert.

They don't convert to becoming social followers. They don't convert to becoming email or podcast subscribers. They don't convert to becoming fans, supporters, or advocates. They don't convert into anything you would want them to become.

As an author, what is the worst part of all those things listed above?

Confused people don't convert to being purchasers or readers of your book.

If you can't clearly establish in someone's mind who you are and why they should care, then they are likely to be confused. And you won't be adding that confused person to your platform.

So what steps can you take to start making sure everything you are doing is clear? What can you be doing proactively to remove potential confusion from the equation?

Try answering these questions:

- Does my current online profile accurately and succinctly describe who I am and what I want to do?

- Could someone who has never heard of me visit my website and my social page, then come back and correctly describe my brand?

- Is my content geared towards my target audience?
- Is there anything I'm saying or writing that could be causing confusion?

Take time when answering these questions. Analyze them from the perspective of someone who has just been introduced to you and your brand. Even consider enlisting someone in your life to help. Ask them to review your content and describe what they are seeing. You need to know what other people are experiencing when they interact with your brand, not just how you perceive your brand to be.

When teaching the craft of writing, Jerry Jenkins always says "Think reader first." He strongly advocates that an author must be thinking of their reader while writing in order for the reader to eventually be reached with the writing.

This applies to building your platform as well. Think of a website visitor first when you are creating your site. Think of a social media follower first when you write your posts. Think of a podcast listener or a YouTube watcher first when you are recording your content.

Making sure you are thinking about your audience first when building your platform will greatly help you to attract the right people to your brand. In this specific case, the *right* people are people who aren't confused. People who want to engage with your material. People who will tell others about what you are doing and how they've enjoyed your stories or how your message has helped them in their life.

Once you've reached this point in creating clarity for your brand, the next step is to make sure you are being consistent across all outlets.

Two caveats to being consistent:

1. Consistent doesn't mean constant

Each outlet you use to build your platform (website, social, email, billboards, etc.) has its own strategy for posting. You have to post every hour or every day, or even every week. What consistent means for you is to decide what your posting schedule or email schedule is going to be, then stick to it. Create trust in the mind of your audience that you will do what you've said you will do. If that means you are sending out a LinkedIn post every weekday morning, great. Do it. If that means you are sending one email each month, awesome. Do it. If it means you are publishing one new podcast every Friday morning, terrific. Do it. Decide what content you can consistently create, and at what frequency you can create it, then go do it. Be committed to consistency. If you want other people to commit themselves to your brand and your content, you need to be determined to commit something to them as well. Commit to be consistent.

2. Consistent doesn't have to mean repetitive

Having a presence in multiple places doesn't mean you need to post the exact same content to each. They are different and should be treated differently. The people following you on Instagram are looking for content best suited to Instagram. They aren't necessarily looking for a repeat of your last tweet, TikTok, or Facebook post.

Some people will read the concepts above and feel the need to be on every app or social site just to make sure they aren't missing anything. If that's you, let's put a stop to that kind of thinking right now!

You don't need to be everywhere. But you do need to be somewhere. And maybe you need to be multiple somewheres. :-)

The point is to find the places where you enjoy spending time engaging online, then find the places where your target audience enjoys engaging online. Once you've listed those out, find the common places between your interests and the interests of your target audience. Then decide which of those you are willing to devote time and energy towards.

From there, it's all about testing your content in the market. Just because you've made a plan doesn't guarantee that plan will work. As you are implementing your plan, watch the results. Take note of where you are when you start (e.g. how many people you are impacting) and run with your plan for 90 days. Then evaluate the results you've achieved in that time period. Measure where you are to where you were previously. If growth is happening and there seems to be room for more growth, keep going. If the results are not meeting your expectations, or if it's clear there isn't any progress of note after that 90 days, it's time to come up with a new plan.

Be willing to create a plan and then test it. But also be ready to make adjustments if that plan proves to be wrong for your brand and audience.

For example, let's say you've decided you are going to participate in both Facebook and on LinkedIn. You've determined that your target audience is active on those platforms and you've also decided you have a personal interest in consistently participating there. Next, answer the following questions:

- How often am I going to post?

Be specific. Is it once per day? Once per week? 10 times per month? Pick a number and a frequency and write it down. Determine now that the schedule you've chosen is non-negotiable for the next 90 days. Give yourself the time to get the most accurate results possible. Pick a schedule and stick to it.

- Because I've decided to stay consistent with this schedule, am I going to create posts in advance or am I going to create new content each time I sit down to post something?

There is no wrong answer here, but you need to determine what works best for your personality. Do you have the time and discipline to sit down on each day you've committed to posting and write something new? It's possible to do, but that approach is difficult to maintain for a lot of people. An alternative to consider is to set aside a block of time each week or month to write several posts. Keep those in a running document that you can easily reference, edit, and add to in the future. When using the term 'running document', we mean something like a Google Doc, Word doc, Notes app, a Pages file, and so on. From that document, you can easily copy and paste the post into the social media platform. Many people find it helpful to then add the date a post was used and the platform it was used on to the document so you can keep track of what material you've used, when it was used, and where it was used.

- What is going to be my strategy for engaging with people on each social platform?

In the example of LinkedIn, part of what currently helps content there to reach more people is the engagement. In this case, engagement includes things like a post having likes *and* comments. If someone sees your post on LinkedIn and takes the time to leave a comment, are you going to reply to that comment? Doing so is a great idea and is something we strongly recommend, but you need to decide what will work for you. Even if replying back to someone's comment is a simple "Thank you, (Name)", we believe it's worth doing. But again, you need to decide what is doable for you. The main point is to make a decision.

- What do I need to do in order to make sure my content and messaging has a consistent feel across all of my selected platforms?

Different social media platforms attract different kinds of people, but you want to make sure your presence feels consistent anywhere people might come in touch with you. If your brand as an author has nothing to do with anything political, be very careful about posting controversial political material on your social pages. That's an extreme example, but we mention it because it happens all the time. Be mindful of the goal you are trying to achieve and be careful to not sabotage yourself by being one person on LinkedIn and a completely different person on Facebook.

- How much time am I going to spend on each of these platforms?

First and foremost, you are an author. You wrote a book because you wanted to write a book and help people or entertain people. Most likely, you didn't set out to write a book so that then you could spend a ton of time on social media trying to build an audience. Our point is this: It is fine that you are primarily an author. But take the time to decide how much of your schedule you are willing to devote to building your audience online. Again, no wrong answer here, but there *does* need to be an answer. Treat this as though the future of your career as an author depends on it. (OK fine, that statement might be hyperbole, but you get the point.) If you treat something as worthless or useless, you are unlikely to ever see any kind of valuable return. But if you treat something with intentionality and care, as though it either is valuable or will become valuable in the future, it is much more likely to yield a return on your investment.

CHAPTER 5:

Developing Your One Sentence

If creating a strategy to be consistent across all outlets is still a daunting task in your mind, it may be because you haven't developed your 'one sentence' yet.

Do you have your 'one sentence'?

We've not seen this concept taught before, though we might be missing the boat. As we were defining our target audience for Leverage, we started to understand that if we couldn't work with an expert who had a one-sentence statement that clearly defined the benefit he or she provided to their target audience, we were missing the boat.

Since that time, we've worked with the following one-sentence brands:

- A husband and wife who help couples overcome infidelity in their marriage and rebuild trust with one another.

- A former executive who helps self starters get unstuck.

- A Grammy-award winning songwriter who helps songwriters write better songs.

And we're on the hunt for a hundred more!

So, if you were asked to describe who you are as an author, what your book is, who it reaches, and why that audience will care … could you answer all of those questions in one sentence?

Here's our most prominent example: Who is Jerry Jenkins?

Jerry is a bestselling author with 200+ books and 73 million copies sold, who continues to write while also teaching the craft of writing online.

Then, use the one sentence to craft your marketing messaging across the site, emails, and even in your book.

Check our work: If an aspiring author finds Jerry's website, what's the first thing they will see?

A statement in big bold letters that says "LET ME HELP YOU WRITE YOUR BOOK".

See how having one sentence helps bring clarity to the audience?

So who are you? Pause right now to think through this question and write down some ideas. Seriously. I'm (David) the guy who rarely pauses when a book tells me to pause. Instead, I want to just keep reading or listening, and I tell myself "Oh, I'll come back to that part later." But I almost never do it. I usually forget because other things come into my mind once I keep going in a book. But I'm working on this, so I challenge you to work on it too. Pause for a moment. Seriously, even just pausing for one minute to ponder this question will help you tremendously in your career.

Who are you?

Write down the first few things that come to your mind when you ask that question.

OK. Back to the book.

Part of the goal here is to determine an answer to this question: What's the first thing someone else will see, read, feel, think, or know when they reach your website or your social page?

There's a lot to digest in that question, but let's focus on two words for now. *Someone else* ... What is someone else going to experience when they come across your brand? This is not about what you think you represent to others. And it's not about what you hope to be representing to others. It's about what someone else is experiencing.

So with that context, read and think about the question again: What's the first thing someone else will see, read, feel, think, or know when they reach your website or social page?

(We'd encourage you to pause again here and write down your thoughts regarding that question, but we realize doing so is probably pushing it!)

***Temptation ALERT**

Back to the concept of your one sentence. Many authors use an excuse here when confronted with the need to boil their life's work into one sentence. Don't do it! Don't fall into the temptation of saying something along the lines of "I can't describe what I do in just one sentence. It's too complicated," or "I do so many things that it would be wrong of me to limit it to just one." Or the worst possible option: "Everyone would benefit from what I'm doing."

It's like the time we met an author who had written a book of over 200,000 words. That's the equivalent of about 800 pages. No agent or publishing company will take a second look at that. It's way too long! In the same way saying, "Everyone would benefit from what you're doing," tells someone like me (Chase, who's been doing this for over a decade) that no one would benefit from what you're doing until you know who you're trying to help.

Think about the absurdity of the statement: *Everyone* would benefit? Really? All of humanity? The billions of people across every continent, if they only were aware of you, would be better off? That's a pretty bold statement. To most who don't know you, saying anything along these lines will come off as arrogant. Tone deaf. Bizarre. Best case would be someone might just be confused by such a statement, and we've already talked about how bad confusion can be.

So if you do have those thoughts, keep them to yourself! But more than that, start shifting your thinking. You might start by saying to yourself, "I think my material could help everyone, but here's the group of people it is most likely to help today."

If that doesn't work, try this: "If I could only have one specific type of person read my book, it would be _____."

Fill in that blank with as much detail and specificity as possible. Age, stage of life, interests, experiences, needs … list them all out. Who is the absolute best person to read what you've written?

This doesn't mean you will always and only reach that type of person with your writing. It just means you are deciding today to start with that kind of person. Start with a target.

Start with that person as the target audience you are aiming towards and then go build your platform around those people. This is why that old cliche, "you've gotta start somewhere" exists. Eventually, you will be able to branch out and capture more people from other demographics, but you can only reach the masses if you've first reached the individuals.

Remind yourself that reaching the masses is step 10. Reaching the individuals in your target audience is step 1. Don't try to skip the steps in between. Delivering value to each person at every step is what will help you get to the next step, and the next, and the next.

This is why having a 'one sentence' for your brand is so important. Let your one sentence be True North for you as you write, as you create content, as you decide what you are going to do.

It's going to take time to craft this. Most of what we do here at Leverage takes more time than most are willing to spend, but having one sentence will actually save time in the long term. Building a platform is tough and there will be countless decisions to make along the way. If you have your one sentence as a guidepost, you'll be able to decide quicker than most as to what your next step should be.

PART II

Starting a Website

Every step in the process that we included to build your platform is crucial to complete prior to starting your website.

Why?

Because the clarity you gain by going through the platform building exercises are immensely helpful in each step of the website development process. They help you inform your choices of how your website works, the user path that you want your customer to take, the complexity of your email marketing, and the frequency of updates that you need. It can even inform your Domain/URL choice.

So, don't skimp on the above steps. If you haven't gone through them step by step, try again. It will make the next technical steps all the more easy, because you won't be second-guessing the targeting choices that you're making.

And now, because you've gone through the steps, you have the tremendous opportunity to do something that established authors (and their digital marketing companies) envy. You have the opportunity to start a new website with such a focused intent that no page will be wasted and no content on accident.

For the established authors we work with, we usually have substantial clean-up efforts that have to take place to get them back to the North Star of their one sentence. Hundreds of posts have to be archived. Dead or old service pages have to be removed. Messaging and opt-ins across the site have to be updated.

You, however, are staring at a clean slate to build an attractive website that acts as a lead capture engine for your target audience.

CHAPTER 6:

Choosing a Domain Name

If you haven't secured a domain for your website prior to this point, you'll need to approach the process with an open mind and potentially alter expectations. People have been able to purchase domains on their own for decades, which means you may have to be creative in how you think about the name of your site.

Start by seeing if your name is available to purchase as a domain. If it is, buy the rights to that domain immediately! Start with .com but also look to see what other top-level domains are available (.net, .biz, .me, .co, etc.)

One note here: In the past having a .com domain name was the standard. However, as more and more extensions (that's the letters after the [dot]) become available, and as links to sites without the user having to type the URL in have become more prevalent, established brands have started to veer from the .com extension. Still, if all are available, grab the .com as that extension is what a user would probably type if they're looking you up on their own.

If you have a unique name you may be able to secure the corresponding domains quickly. If your name is commonly used in society, it is likely no longer available for purchase. But don't worry, you still have options!

If your name isn't available to purchase as a domain, try these alternatives:

- Add your middle initial (First NameMiddleInitialLastName)
- Add your full middle name (FirstNameMiddleNameLastName)

- Add the word *author* before your first name (AuthorFirstNameLastName)

- Add the word *author* after your last name (FirstNameLastNameAuthor)

- Add the word *the* before your first name (TheFirstNameLastName)

- Consider words like says, writes, teaches, or stories to add after your last name (FirstNameLastNameTeaches)

This is the time to get creative. Having a memorable domain will help establish you as a brand in the minds of your audience, so don't skip over this step.

If you are still struggling to find the right domain, you can consider looking for the title of your book and making that your domain. But this should be a last resort. Exhaust all efforts to secure a domain that is based around your name as an author before you consider switching to the title of your book.

Why? Because you are trying to build continuity with your audience. You are the author. You are the expert. You are the creator of this content. You are the brand. Build that brand around your name if at all possible. If you are an author, you are likely planning to write more than one book. So having your website named after your first book won't make sense when your second or third or fourth books are completed.

A few exceptions to this general rule include if:

- You are running a nonprofit organization

- You are pastoring a church

- You are writing a book on behalf of another entity
- You are creating a legacy-based brand that is bigger than you individually, will exist long after you do, and/or has other contributing personalities and voices

In those cases, a domain based around the cause or the name of the group you represent might be the best choice. But think through the details and the potential pros and cons before you make a final decision to go this direction. We generally advise that a domain should, by default, include the author's name unless there is an obvious reason not to do so.

Remember, the domain name is a critical building block, but it's not unchangeable. So, even if you pick a domain name that you end up wanting to change in the future (either because another one becomes available or you're looking to rebrand), you can change it. Make the best choice for today following these general guidelines, but (and this will be a refrain throughout) don't let perfection get in the way of progress.

Closing Note about the future of websites, domains, and online consumption in general

While it is likely the way we access websites will change in the future, it is important for authors to participate in what exists in the marketplace today. There's been talk for years about how websites as we know them will eventually go away, and the method for people to access content online will change drastically. That is likely true, but it is not the reality we operate in currently. Don't use the likelihood of future internet changes as an excuse to do nothing today. Don't wait for the next wave of technology before you jump in. Take action now and then be ready to adjust as things change in the future.

And keep apprised of what's going on. There's always a wave of new influencers when new social media and blogging/podcasting platforms come out, and depending on the platform, those influencers may have staying power—think YouTube influencers vs. influencers on Vine (remember Vine?) So, that may be a way to jumpstart the whole platform building process, but it's certainly not a reason to not get started today with a website as a home base.

CHAPTER 7:

Architecting Your Website

Architecting can seem like a truly insurmountable obstacle because it sounds like an insurmountable process.

It's not.

Just as an architect draws plans for the house, a web architect draws wireframes to help you understand how the user will interact with your site. The prime thing to remember here is that it is better to keep it simple than to try to plan for every contingency in the first go around.

At a minimum, the architecture should give your end user the ability to learn the following things:

- Who you are

- How you can help them

- What next step to take

We'll take each of these in turn.

<u>Who you are:</u>

Generally, this is on an 'about' page, but on some single page websites, it's a simple paragraph. The 'who you are' page should tell the user your credentials for helping them along their path and instill in them the trust that you have their best interest at heart.

It should not be a list of accomplishments only. Nor should it only serve as a billboard for your puffed up resume. Instead, state clearly what makes you the best expert online for the subject matter involved.

Here's an example from our self-publishing brand, TheSelfPublisher.com:

I'll Show You How to Make a Living as an Author

Making a living selling your books sounds like some crazy pipe dream.

It seems like you either have to be the next J. K. Rowling or get extremely lucky to have the opportunity to become a full-time author.

But is that really true?

Absolutely not.

I make a livable income off my writing, and I know plenty of other authors who do the same.

So why do so many people believe this myth?

Because they expect to make 6 figures off their books within a year.

They've heard crazy success stories of people making millions off their self-published books ...

They've heard wild claims that say if you follow certain strategies, you can whip together a book and make thousands of dollars within a matter of months ....

And because of all the noise, they set unreasonably high expectations.

I'm here to make sure you don't fall into the same trap.

My name is C.S. Lakin, and I'm a full-time author, blogger, editor, and writing coach. I've written and published 30+ books over the last 10 years and make a comfortable income from my writing.

I work with writers all over the world, and they tell me their stories of success and failure. I've interviewed literary agents, publishers, and best-

selling authors to learn what tips they have for authors wanting to make a living from their writing.

I'm bringing more than 30 years of experience and wisdom gleaned from the ups and downs of my writing journey to this website.

I started The Self-Publisher to help you make a comfortable income from your books too.

Because I firmly believe that if you love writing, are dedicated to improving your craft, and persevere, you can get to a spot where you can make writing your full-time paying job.

You might not become a millionaire ...

You might not become the next Stephen King ...

You might not have tens of thousands of fans waiting on pins and needles for your next book ...

But you can reach the point where you can pay your bills doing what you love most (not to mention the freedom to go to work in your PJs and bunny slippers!).

There are simple, practical methods to building your career as a self-publishing author. Yes, it takes work and time. No, you're not going to be rich overnight. But seeing progress and success grow incrementally is both encouraging and exciting.

I've seen my writing career take off in ways I could never have imagined. I believe you can experience this success too!

I hear from writers all the time who have followed these tried-and-true methods to successful self-publishing and are psyched by their book sales and growing fan base.

I'm here to help you make that dream a reality for you too.

You see how that focuses on the person who is coming to the site rather than the expert. We don't even talk about C.S. Lakin until halfway down the page. That's the ideal way to tell your website user about who you are.

How you can help them:

Now that you've established your trust, what services or products can you deliver to the end user that unlikely helps them get from where they are to where they want to be?

As an author, many times, there's a book that takes the end user down several steps of their journey to becoming who they want to become. As an online business owner, like David and me, sometimes these "helps" come in the way of services instead. Regardless, you need to show them the unique value you can provide to them and why they should choose your service or products over the other ones available to you.

What next step to take:

This is the call to action. Now that you've presented your case as to why these folks should trust you and why they should use your service or product, it is time for you to give the user an actionable way to take that next step. It could be as simple as giving them the opportunity to continue the conversation by giving their email for something of value (we call this a lead magnet). It could also be a consultation call to engage your services.

Make sure that the next step matches the thing that they are after. The worst thing you can do is to make assumptions about the next step that aren't truly what your end user wants. That's why the research you've done above is so critical.

On the Jerry Jenkins website, we handle the *How We Can Help* and *What Next Step to Take* sections in a single lead magnet call on his home page:

What's holding back your writing? Take this free assessment now and learn to unlock your true potential:
[BUTTON] Take the FREE Writing Assessment

But we also walk through these same steps on each page of his website. In the same way, each page of your website should take the user through each of these as they browse the site.

If your 'about' page isn't giving your target audience a clear next step, then it's failing its purpose on your website. Similarly, if a blog post doesn't clearly communicate how you can help the target audience, then you've missed the boat. Each element of your site needs to be intentional, just like each word of your book is there for a reason.

As an author, you already have a proclivity to paying this much attention to detail—use that skill to make your website an amazing resource and an amazing lead engine for your career.

CHAPTER 8:

Above the Fold

In your website architecting process, one thing to keep in mind is the most important section on your home page—the above-the-fold area.

This is an old newspaper term. Imagine a day's newspaper in one of those old newsstands. You know, the ones that you paid a quarter for. Except on Sundays. That sucker was four quarters. The Sunday comics were totally worth it though!

Anyway, the front page on those papers was folded in half. That top section is "above the fold." Similarly, your website has an above-the-fold section. It's the section at the top of the homepage that users see before the first scroll occurs. This is your chance to shine. It's your opportunity to capture someone's attention and keep them engaged. Your goal is to have them continue reading or clicking, but to do that, you must make excellent use of the above-the-fold section.

At most, you have fifteen seconds to clearly communicate with your website visitor and many studies say you have even less time than that. Don't be scared by this reality. Instead, use the facts to help sharpen your message.

The above-the-fold section is crucial no matter what device is being used to view it. Mobile, desktop, laptop, whatever else … it applies to any way someone can be viewing your site. So, you need to make sure that area of your site clearly communicates the three sections that we covered already. Remember, this is the gateway for people to eventually see the entirety of your website.

Specifically, your above-the-fold section should cover:

Who you are

How you can help them

What next step to take (sound familiar?)

Generally, this is accomplished by a headline, a subheadline and a call to action. Most author sites also include a pretty picture of the author, though that's not 100 percent necessary.

Use that one sentence you've developed to make this super clear (and then clarify with your sub-headline). You'll notice that these start to stack on top of each other with "who you are" adding to "how you can help." Here are a few examples from our recent work:

Let me help you write your book. *potential:*

Let me help you become a better songwriter. *songs.*

Believe more is possible. *clarity?*

Let's look at the Jerry Jenkins example a little more closely: the headline, for instance, is *Let Me Help You Write Your Book.*

This clearly communicates how he can help the user. For anyone who is interested in the craft of writing, that headline is going to draw their attention immediately and keep them reading.

[Important reminder: Jerry's target audience is authors and people who want to learn how to write. His headline is targeted directly to that audience. Your target audience is almost certainly different from Jerry's, so make sure your headline speaks right to the core of what your people want.]

Next, use a clear call to action that tells them the next step. Again, using Jerry as an example, he says: What's holding back your writing? Take this free assessment now and learn to unlock your true potential.

Again, we are addressing how he can help (unlocking their potential) and then giving a clear next step (take the assessment). As an added bonus, it's free.

Finally, it has to communicate who he is. In the subhead for Jerry, we use "21-Time New York Times Bestselling Author Jerry Jenkins Reveals His Secrets."

Granted, that statement of success about what Jerry has accomplished results in immediate authority and subject matter expertise. Your statement might not carry that same weight yet, but that is fine. When you are clear on how you can help your audience, you will find that your qualifications follow along the path. Out of your passion and experience comes the value you bring to others.

It could be as simple as you walking with the audience as you figure out something together. Or it could be as clear as Jerry's, where you are the ultimate authority on your specific topic. But you have to make sure that above-the-fold area is a microcosm of the whole website.

Go through the other examples provided above (we've linked them for your convenience). Can you see how we've used the same framework to bring authority to those sites as well?

Now, start thinking about how your above-the-fold section can accomplish these things for you. Doing so will produce results for your website just like they're driving links and traffic for the examples listed above.

CHAPTER 9:

Tech Stack

Above, you read that you need to have a call to action. That might be a new term for you. But think about it this way:

When users come to your website, what's the one action that you want them to take?

The answer to that question should inform what your call to action is. It could be as simple as signing up for an email list. It could be as complex as booking a consultation call with you to help them with content writing needs or editing, or whatever expertise you've discovered you can speak to and that others may pay you to do for them.

Regardless of the call to action, however, you must have the technical systems in place to capture that user and his or her information in order for you to take the next step in your relationship with that person.

These technical systems are commonly referred to as a *tech stack*. It is really just the sum total of the technology assets you are using that help to maintain your presence online.

We are frequently asked about the tech stack that makes user interactions with Jerry Jenkins possible. So, let us go ahead and lay out the list we've used in the past before we built some custom solutions. CAUTION: This list will overwhelm you (and that's on purpose), especially because of how many acronyms are used. But don't worry, some of the more important acronyms will be explained in the coming paragraphs. Others are easy to read more about if you are interested in doing a quick online search. For now, just read through this list and become aware of the terms.

CMS (Content Management Software)

Wordpress

CRM (Customer Relationship Manager)

Infusionsoft: *Customer communication (broadcast and transactional), subscription services, and business automation*

Payment Processing

Stripe: *Payment gateway*

Nexus Merchants: *Infusionsoft-to-Stripe connection*

Hosting and Services

WP Engine: *Managed Wordpress hosting*

Cloudflare: *Content Delivery Network (CDN), security, Domain Name System (DNS), and performance tools*

Mailgun: *Wordpress-generated transactional email delivery*

Google via Google Tag Manager (GTM): *Tag manager, analytics, optimization, and webmaster tools*

Hotjar: *User engagement reporting and visualization*

Github: *Code repository and version tracking*

Design

Invision: *Interactive, clickable prototype delivery*

Zeplin: *Asset management and design handoff*

Essential Plugins

Memberium: *Infusionsoft-integrated Membership site control*

Learndash: *Online course platform (LMS)*

Buddypress: *Social network enablement*

BB Press: *Forums platform*

Gravity Forms: *Form management with developer framework options*

Beaver Builder: *Page builder functionality*

Advanced Custom Fields: *Custom form management*

Essential Theme

Understrap: *Custom AG-developed theme built on WP Underscores and Bootstrap 4*

Marketing Plugins

Thrive Leads: *Lead generation and reporting*

Now that you've seen the list, let's take a look through a few of the key pieces. Once you understand the functions of each element, then you can start making decisions based on how you will interact with your users.

1. **Hosting and CMS**

Your hosting and Content Management Software (CMS) are the foundation of your website build. Very few people will know what these are for your particular site, but the choice is crucial to you. Why? Based on what you choose here, you will be able to edit your site very easily or very difficulty.

Our suggestion is to keep it simple. Wordpress is a foundational CMS for content creators that doesn't seem to be going anywhere. It's free, and it is fairly user-friendly.

For the pieces that aren't user-friendly, there's bunch of plugins that make it more user-friendly (like Beaver Builder, mentioned above as a webpage builder).

For hosting, you have a myriad of options. For some who are more technical savvy, you may choose a simple host like Hostgator. For others who want a little more support, something like Bluehost would be better.

Wordpress Engine is what we use because we are committed to Wordpress as our CMS, and we need an enterprise solution.

For an easy start, check out Jerry's post on starting an author website, which recommends Bluehost and Wordpress:

https://jerryjenkins.com/author-website/

2. CRM

Now that you've set up the foundation of your website, you need to choose a Customer Relationship Management Software (CRM). There are a bunch of options here as well, so as you consider what to use, we'd keep the following factors in mind:

      a. Ease of setup and use

      b. Cost

      c. Scale-ability

Choosing a CRM can become quite the commitment, so you want to make sure that you're choosing the right one for your situation. As a starting point, consider free options like MailChimp. Mailchimp has a hefty free tier that will allow you to build the beginning of an email list without the burden of a monthly payment (at first). Then as you grow, you might decide you need something a little more robust in its options for automation, integration, and outreach to your end user. That will lead you down the road to software like Keap, ActiveCampaign, Convertkit, and more.

These are each solid options with pros and cons, so do your research. When you start adding automation, you're adding complexity. When you add complexity, you add buy-in to the platform because getting out of the platform becomes more difficult.

We've put together a brief review of these in our post on tools you might use to build your platform here:

https://leveragecreativegroup.com/branding-tools/

3. <u>Other Tools</u>

After you've selected these cornerstone elements of your tech stack (CMS, CRM, and hosting) the decision on the other tools that you need becomes much easier. You need tools that will natively integrate with the tech stack you've built. So, as you're researching what you need, make sure that you check into its ability to integrate with everything else. If it does, then you're good to go, but be sure to confirm the integration before proceeding.

Some overlooked tools that will be crucial to adding early on:

<u>Google Analytics</u>: You have to know how people are using your website if you want to grow your brand. Google Analytics is the most applicable tool for this.

<u>On-demand Staff</u>

Fiverr. If you don't have the funds to hire a graphic designer, Fiverr can be a good solution. Make sure the designs don't infringe on other artists' work, though.

Upwork. Another marketplace for freelancers. We've found web experts, bookkeepers, marketing consultants, and more on this site.

99 Designs. Another option for on-demand graphic artists, whether you're creating a new product logo or looking for a designer for a book cover for your new lead magnet.

Here's a word of caution on website building: There are so many opinions out there about this, and there are a thousand ways to build it. So, make sure that you're not getting caught in the paralysis of analysis as you're building your site.

Pick a path, and move forward. Don't try to be perfect—get something out there to start building some authority on your platform, especially as you prepare for your book launch. Make something that you're proud of, and then move on to more pressing matters—like finding readers for your book!

PART III

Planning a Book Launch

We've spent an awful lot of time on topics prior to covering the core of author marketing—the book launch. You may be thinking that's a mistake, or maybe you haven't even thought of the book launch process yet, or you may have skipped everything else to get here. If that's you, welcome to the book! We are glad to have you here, but we still suggest reading through the previous pages when you are able. :-)

The first two sections are foundational to planning your book launch so don't neglect the material covered to this point. Part I (Building a Platform) and Part II (Starting a Website) are both crucial steps. The sooner you get them set up, the sooner your brand will start benefiting from each one.

Remember how we talked previously about not skipping steps on your journey? This is another example of that same principle.

Still not convinced? Then play along with the following scenario. Think about this potential interaction: You are attending a writer's conference and you have the opportunity to meet with an industry expert about your book. The conversation goes something like this:

Agent/Publisher: Can you send me a query letter for your book?

You: Absolutely. I can email you a document this weekend when I get home from the conference.

Agent/Publisher: Wonderful. I'll be watching for that to show up in my inbox. In the meantime, I'd like to review your website and your social pages to get a better feel for who you are as an author and personality.

You: Well, my website is "under construction" at the moment and I haven't found my footing on any social platform yet.

Agent/Publisher: Oh, well, actually hold off on sending that query letter. We are currently only reviewing submissions from authors who have an established website and/or social media following. Get back to me once your material is ready for review.

Yikes! That's a golden opportunity that was lost, and it has absolutely nothing to do with the quality of your writing. The connection is potentially ruined because you don't have the foundations of your brand put together.

Now compare that conversation to this one. Same scenario, but a different outcome:

Agent/Publisher: Can you send me a query letter for your book?

You: Absolutely. I can have that to you in a week. In the meantime, if you'd like to learn more about me, please take a look at my website [myname].com where I post frequently about this topic. I'm also active on (pick a social media platform) if you want to follow me there.

Agent/Publisher: Sounds good! We are always interested in working with authors who are actively building their following. I'll review your website and I'll watch for your email.

That's a much better ending to the conversation, right? Will giving them the website and your social pages guarantee that they will look at it and sign you to a deal? Absolutely not, but it does prove that you are invested in these efforts. They will know you took the prerogative to build a platform on your own, and that they're not starting from square one if they decide to work with you. They would much rather work with an author who is clearly putting in the time and effort outside of just writing the book than work with an author who is expecting someone else to do all the work for them. Decide now which you are going to be.

Publishing is a business and you are the brand. Your book is the product. You have to figure out ways to make your brand and your product appealing to both potential purchasers and the people who help to facilitate the transactions—in this case, the publishing industry. If you come to the table with a website, a social strategy, a personality, and a willingness to work hard, then you are setting yourself up for the best chance to succeed.

OK. So now we've finally convinced you of the importance of Parts I and II of this book. Once you have those assets created, you'll be well positioned to start planning your book launch.

CHAPTER 10:

Self Publishing or Traditional Publishing

Should I self-publish my book or try to have it published traditionally?

It's a question authors have been asking for a long time. Beyond asking, it's a question that has resulted in more opinions, rants, and arguments than just about anything else in the publishing industry. Before we continue, please read and remember this statement:

This is not a good-guy vs. bad-guy scenario. Both options have unique value to bring to authors, but there are many misconceptions about each side. Every author should be fully informed about the potential benefits and risks associated with both traditional and self publishing.

When talking about self-publishing vs. traditional publishing, it's important to start with two basic pieces of information.

1. Traditional publishing is an established business model, but not all books published by the big publishers are profitable—and certainly not all authors who are traditionally published are great writers.

2. Self-publishing is an established business model, but the structure of that model is notably different from traditional publishing.

These statements are odd for many authors to hear, but it's worth thinking through the specifics of each and understanding all the contributing factors before deciding which route is best for you. Let's analyze both of these statements in-depth.

1. Traditional publishing is an established business model but not all books published by the big publishers are profitable—and certainly not all authors who are traditionally published are great writers.

Not every book published by a traditional publisher is financially viable. That might seem like an obvious statement but it's worth remembering. An executive at one of the big houses recently told us that their company projects for 30-33 percent of the titles they will publish this year to carry the entire company financially. For the baseball fans out there, you already know where this is headed. It means the publisher expects and plans around the fact that if they can hit .333 this year, they will be doing great! They expect to "strike out" on up to 70 percent of the projects they publish. Think about that!

It makes sense though. For every single book published by those companies to be a huge financial success, they would have to have a flawless fortune teller on their staff. It's good for authors to remind themselves that even publishing companies who are experts at what they do, still miss. But they plan for it. And they know that when they do get a hit, it's going to carry everything else.

Now of course, they don't know which books will be in the 30 percent category and which will be in the 70 percent. They believe in every project they produce and they give it their best effort, but at the end of the day, it is the public who determines the success of a book. It's the readers who love a book so much they have to tell their friends about it. Publishers can guess and project and predict, and they are often right. They can influence what the market does, but they can't dictate it.

The second part of that first statement (not all authors who are traditionally published are great writers) is another layer to the issue. Just because someone is able to secure a deal with a traditional publisher doesn't mean they are outstanding at the craft of writing. People get publishing deals for all kinds of reasons, some having nothing to do with their actual competency of a writer. In a perfect world, the best writers would get the best and biggest publishing deals. But the world—and the publishing industry as a whole—is far from perfect.

2. Self-publishing is also an established business model but the structure of that model is notably different from traditional publishing.

For an author to understand which publishing option is best for their book, it helps to fully understand the differences between traditional and self-publishing. One difference is a traditional publisher isn't charging an author for any services, whereas a self-publishing company charges the author a fee to perform a myriad of services related to the book, like its creation, distribution, and so on.

Another key difference is a higher level of quality control from traditional publishers vs. self- publishing. As mentioned above, not every traditionally published book is of the highest quality of writing, but they do have a process in place to vet submissions and determine what writings have the best chance at commercial success. Traditional publishers have divisions and imprints teams of people focused on specific genres. Their editors keep tabs on what the market in that genre is doing, what readers are liking, what trends exist and what other trends might be coming in the future. Self-publishing companies may have some of these elements, but for the most part, they lack a rigid quality assurance system for the books they represent.

This brings us to another topic that is likely to ruffle feathers: The term "self-publishing" itself.

Sadly, the term was coined long before this book was written, but let us take the opportunity to say what someone should've said a long time ago.

It should not be called self-publishing.

The term is inaccurate and misleading. Whoever created the term did a great job at trying to connect something to publishing that really isn't publishing. Publishing implies that a work has been reviewed, considered, edited, accepted, purchased, and is believed in by a team of people. Self-publishing is riding the coattails of the term publishing and attempting to make the general audience believe they are essentially the same thing.

They are not. This won't happen, but the entire industry would likely benefit from the name "self- publishing" going away completely. Potential names to consider (once society acknowledges this error and convenes a board to vote) are:

- Pay to Print
- Self production
- Self-employed printer
- Entre-print-eur (okay fine, this one probably goes too far but it made us laugh to type it!)

You get the point though. There really isn't much "publishing" going on for someone using a self-publisher. But when the names are similar, it leads to misconceptions about both sides.

Here are a few more key elements to keep in mind when thinking about what separates self- publishing from traditional:

- If you are an author and you are using a self-publishing service, you are essentially paying someone to print your book. A traditional publisher takes on the financial risk of printing and distributing a book and pays the author a royalty based on the sales generated (an advance on those royalties is often added as well as an enticement from the publisher to the author prior to the manuscript being completed).

- Many (but not all) self publishing companies will print whatever an author sends to them. If someone is willing to pay to have their entire family genealogy printed in hardback with full color headshots of each family member, the self-publishing company will do it. They know it won't sell, but they don't care because the author is paying them regardless of sales results. The same concept applies to any other form of manuscript. Whether it's good or bad, relevant or useless, timely or outdated, interesting or boring ... if someone pays the required fees then many self-publishing companies will print the book.
  There is nothing wrong with this being true, provided the author fully understands the reality of the market they are entering.

- A traditional publisher is only printing and distributing the books they believe they can sell in the market. They have a team of acquisition editors, sales reps, and marketers who review each potential book and determine if they believe it can be a profitable project. If they see red flags during their evaluation process of working with a potential author and book, they will either fix those issues or terminate the project completely.

- A traditional publisher is going to bring a full team to the table for the books they represent. They will handle everything on the front end from the contract to the manuscript deadline schedule, from the editorial and review process to the sales strategy, from the distribution partners to the marketing plan, the typesetting, the printing, the shipping, the fulfillment, the returns, buybacks, bulk discounts, audiobook creation, ebook creation, paperbacks, 2nd editions, revisions, and on and on. They provide all these elements because they are financially invested with the author to make the book work if possible. They win when the author wins. They lose if the author loses. It's a risk for a traditional publisher to take on any book. They must sell books in order for it to work, but they have a team of proven experts who will give each book a chance to succeed.

- A self-published book often has the author doing everything listed in the bullet point above. In addition to needing to write a great book, the author then needs to turn into an editor, designer, marketer, publicist, salesperson, fulfillment specialist, and so on. The author can pay the self-publishing company to do certain components, but that in itself is vastly different from what a traditionally published author does.

- Royalty percentages is another common misconception. Yes, the traditional publishing royalties are lower than self-publishing. Traditional deals are likely to be in the 7-17 percent range for first-time authors, potentially higher if there is no advance. Or in a few other specific situations, self-publishing royalties can be 60-80 percent. On its face, the gap between those numbers is huge. But if you pause to think about the reason why the gap exists in the first place, things start to make sense. For traditional houses, they pay lower royalties because they are also paying their staff to do all the other things that must be done for a book to work. Self-publishing pays higher royalties because they don't have the staff and overhead to pay in those areas. The author is the one taking on those tasks. It's best for authors to not get distracted by the royalty disparity. Instead, analyze the potential cost of doing work solo vs. having a team do the work on the author's behalf.

Jerry Jenkins often says, "Do you want to be paid to be published? Or do you want to pay to be printed?" That is a great question every author should consider. And there is no wrong answer here, but if you go into the decision having all pertinent facts available, then you'll give yourself the best chance to make the right choice.

There are absolutely times to choose self-publishing. In fact, there are some situations where you should likely start with self-publishing and ignore traditional options. A few examples include:

- If you have a desire to move quickly (or at least faster than the speed of a standard traditionally published book moves)

- If your ultimate goal is to simply have a finished book in your hands and none of the other details of sales, the publishing industry, or public reception really matter

- If you are writing something for your family or friends only, and you realize there is likely not mass market potential for your book

- If you already have an existing audience of potential purchasers and you don't want or need help in finding more

- If you are eager to be the final word on content and other consequential elements

- If you have the skillset to not only write a great book, but also oversee cover design, layout, back cover copy, sales copy, and marketing copy

- If you have a desire to be in control of everything going on with a book

If these statements describe where you are, self-publishing is likely the way to go.

It can also be a helpful process for authors to go through the process of attempting traditional publishing. Doing so will give the author a real sense of how their manuscript compares with the rest of the market. If an author can survive going through the process of getting a literary agent for representation, and/or getting a publishing company to give them a traditional deal, then that author has accomplished something notable.

In most cases, we advise authors to exhaust their options in traditional publishing before making a decision on self-publishing. Write a great book. Create a great proposal. Pitch your material to agents and acquisitions editors. See what professionals in the industry say about your writing and then decide how to proceed.

CHAPTER 11:

Book Marketing Timeline

A proven and successful author came to us several years ago and said, "I want to hire your company immediately to help with my book launch. What will it cost and when can you start?"

Cue the cha-ching noises of a cash register in your head, right? Let's goooo! Applebee's is on me tonight!

Right?! Not so fast. Let's tap the brakes on that "Fancy Like" scenario (it's a song by Walker Hayes for those of you who are furrowing your brow and tilting your head right now. Go watch and listen on YouTube!)

Having a proven author approach us with this offer might sound like a great opportunity for an online author marketing company like ours, but we quickly learned there was more to the situation than what appeared on the surface.

We went through our standard list of evaluation questions and the answers we received started revealing several red and yellow flags about the project.

The author had written several books prior to this one, but had recently been advised he needed a new marketing team and was looking for someone to step in and help quickly.

The book was scheduled to come out in less than two months, and the author was convinced it had the potential to be a bestseller.

Our response was not an immediate "no," but we did feel the need to point out our concerns about the author's expectations. Less than two months is not enough to create and execute a book marketing plan, even for an established and proven author. Think about other product launches or commercial efforts. Could any of those be expected to execute at a high level on such a short timeline? Can a business be created and launched and successful in less than two months? Unlikely.

So for a book, there isn't an answer that fits every situation. But when thinking about the timing for marketing a book and putting a plan in place that gives the best chance of success, the default answer should be, as early in the process as possible.

Optimally, authors will have a minimum of nine months lead time before a book releases. We've worked on projects with 18 months' notice and while having that much time isn't essential, it certainly helps in terms of creating a plan that allows time to gather potential purchasers, nurture them with valuable content, and lead them to a point where they are primed to receive the sales pitch of the book.

People don't usually respond well to being sold on their first interaction with an author, a book, or a brand. It takes several touchpoints for someone to go from being a cold lead to being warm and ready to buy. So the more time an author has to work with an audience and help move them from cold to warm, the better.

If you only have six weeks to turn people from cold to warm, the chances are much lower than if you had nine months. The shorter your marketing timeline is, the lower you should expect your conversation percentage to be.

Back to the author who approached us needing help quickly. He heard us out when we described our concerns and he seemed to agree with our reasoning. We told him it would be best to treat the real book release date as a "soft launch" because generating results that quickly would be unlikely. We suggested the author shift his mindset and aim for a new date many months out and to start treating that date as the measuring stick for when results could be achieved.

Obviously we are biased, but the plan we put forth to the author was solid. It gave the author a way to attract new people to his platform. Once people were engaged with his brand, they would be walked through a series of free blog posts, emails, and other valuable content. The sequence would then give those new people the best chance to purchase the book over time. The plan would work if the author would agree to devote the amount of time that was required.

So what happened?

Come on … you already know, right? The author accepted our plan and ended up selling millions of copies of his book.

WRONG.

The author seemed to understand our reasoning at a head-level, but in his heart, he couldn't separate the release date of his book (the one with less than two months of prep) from the proposed new date we suggested for when results could be expected.

Expectations were already set in his mind and there wasn't room for those to be adjusted. Neither were we willing to adjust our projections for what was likely to be possible in that timeline.

So we did not work on the project. The author, who is still successful and prominent today, decided to go a different direction for that specific book. The book in question ended up selling very few copies at its release. It went on to be a moderate success in the coming years, but the author and publisher both felt it never reached its potential.

Had the author followed our suggested plan, we believe it's likely the book would've experienced more success than it did, but that is pure speculation.

But beyond speculation is the fact that the author and whoever he ended up using for a marketing team were working on an extremely limited timeline—an unnecessarily short timeline. That timeline and the author's choice to follow it, offered zero benefit to the overall project efforts and it put a ceiling on the impact potential of the book. We (and we assume the author and publisher) look back at that situation and wonder, "What could that have accomplished if...?"

The point of this story is to maximize whatever time is available leading up to a book being released. Writing a great book is the top priority. Don't skimp on the quality of the writing, but once that is done make sure to give appropriate and realistic time to the marketing side of the project.

It is extremely difficult to write a book. Many people talk about writing, but few actually follow through and make it happen, to the point of a completed manuscript. If you are one of those who actually completes the process, don't stop there. Think through the next steps necessary to market the book.

If your goal is to reach a lot of people with your book and sell as many copies as possible, it is reasonable to expect doing so will take a lot of time and effort. The book publishing industry isn't for those who want quick results with only a small amount of energy put forth. Plan as far in advance as possible. Give your book every opportunity to reach the desired audience. Don't cut corners in the process. Every corner you cut is full of potential customers who are being eliminated from contention. Don't eliminate those people just because you wanted to move faster or because you didn't want to put in the work to bring them into your content.

Think of how long it has taken you (or will eventually take you) to finish writing your manuscript. Your book marketing strategy deserves at least as much time as your writing process, and in most cases, the marketing side actually deserves more time because it involves more people and more moving parts.

Below is a list of essential steps when you are planning a book marketing timeline:

1. Decide early in your book writing process what you are wanting to accomplish once the book is completed

2. Set a pub-date or release date for the book

3. Determine how far in advance you start the audience building process and the marketing efforts for the book

4. Remind yourself that the process of marketing a book takes time. The more time you have to plan, the better.

5. Choose whether you will be the responsible party for creating and implementing the marketing plan for the book, or if an outside entity will be tasked with those efforts.

Further, as an example book marketing plan timeline, check out the attached from a recent book proposal (you'll notice that the deadlines start 12 months out):

Marketing Plan Example (which Leverage has used with successful book campaigns previously)

12 months before

- Website development with literary agency or other partners

- Research target audience (where are they active online, what other books are they reading, what problems are they facing that can be helped or solved by this new book)

6 months before

- Develop media kit (digital only or digital and physical, decide on content to include)
- Finalize book cover
- Get endorsements to use in marketing efforts
- New headshots to use on book cover, website, in media kit
- Create book landing page with a lead magnet
- Guest podcast research and outreach
- Guest blog research and outreach

3 months before

- Set up pre-order campaign funnel
- Decide on timing and placement for where pre-orders can happen
- Run ads to landing page

1 month before

- Write and finalize launch emails for email subscribers (customized to email)
- Write and finalize launch posts for social (customized to social)

- Schedule release of guest blogs and guest podcasts, and coordinate promotion of each into both email and social posting calendars

- Prepare launch event at local bookstore, church, chamber, etc. (Attendees who purchase a book receive a photo with author and author will sign each book at the event)

- Create a bulk purchase campaign offering discounts to groups who purchase by the case (determine what quantity of purchases merits a bulk discount, decide target groups to approach with the discounted offer)

Week of launch

- Push for reviews from email list

- Reminders for bulk purchase campaign

- Celebrate the launch on social media with pictures, videos, and text posts

1 month after

- Gather testimonials from readers (written, audio, and video if possible) and organize them all in a filing system to be referenced in the future

3 months after

- Release several of the best testimonials from readers on social media, in email, on video, etc. as social proof of the quality of the content. This soft sell approach gives a great way to keep mentioning the book and its benefits without asking people to purchase directly

6 months after

- Secondary sales push to sustain product life (similar content to the week of launch can be used but should be revisited and updated accordingly)
- Reach out to all potential bulk purchase customers again

12 months after

- Determine secondary products based on the book with continued development. Examples of secondary products include things like:
    - A sequel if the book was a novel, or spinoff short story of one of the main characters
    - Follow-up book on a tangential topic if the book was nonfiction
    - Coaching session with the author
    - Online course
    - A monthly membership offering where readers can interact with the author online

At this point, if you're anything like us, you're feeling two things:

1. Completely overwhelmed
2. Excited about the possibilities of your book launch

That's good! It's a lot of work to make a book launch successful, and we want to be sure that you're absolutely and totally prepared for it. So, let's dive into some of the particulars here to give you a head start on where to start.

CHAPTER 12:

Building a List of Potential Influencers/Partners

There are really two components that we will want to cover extensively in this chapter. The first is the how—how to approach potential influencers and partners. The second is the who—which influencers should you approach in the first place, and how to find them.

Let's start with the theory, and then dive into the tactics after that.

How to approach specific influencers

A crucial piece to the influence puzzle is learning how to approach each target. Timing, style, tone of the outreach, frequency of communication, and knowing your desired outcome should all be taken into account.

If you are able to reach out to an influencer directly, great! But many times, you'll find you need to go through someone else on their team (manager, assistant, gatekeeper, etc.) before being able to connect directly with your target. Having been the primary gatekeeper for numerous influencers, our team has developed some strategies that will help in navigating these conversations.

First, you need to come up with your target list to contact. We'll talk more about how to define your target in the next section.

Next, spend dedicated time researching each person you plan to contact. It's easy to follow the influencers themselves online, but you might have to also look into their staff. Many gatekeepers list their job title on places like LinkedIn, so you might need to spend time researching those profiles also.

Watch what they are doing on social media. Sign up for their email list (or the email list of the influencer they represent) and pay attention to the communication strategy they are using. Read the blog posts on their website. Listen to interviews the influencer has done on podcasts or radio. Watch some of their YouTube videos. All of these things take time, but it will give you information to help in your effectiveness when the time comes to reach out and hopefully interact with each person.

Then you'll want to decide the method and timing of how to engage. After you've studied their brand and where they are spending time, and once you get a feel for where they are active, you'll start to see the places that might be best to start a conversation. It might be through an email or a contact form on their website. It could be through DMs on Twitter, or maybe by connecting on LinkedIn. But you won't know where to start unless you are watching what that influencer and/or their gatekeeper is doing.

Once you've selected the method of outreach, think through the timing that could work best. Is that person active on a social site around the same time each weekday? If so, consider sending your message then.

If you are dealing with a gatekeeper, email, or a contact form, sending messages first thing in the morning in the middle of the week can be a great place to start. Why? Because people's inboxes are usually flooded on Monday mornings, so your message might get lost in the volume. And people are eager to close things out on Fridays (many of us block Fridays completely and avoid meetings or new messages completely if possible in order to wrap up everything else from the week).

When you reach out to a gatekeeper, remember they are holding the keys to the door you want to open. Keep these tips in mind:

- Be friendly. Don't say anything to a gatekeeper that you wouldn't say to the influencer directly. Give yourself the opportunity to build a relationship with this person. Even if they don't engage with you the first time, you never want to burn a bridge between you and them.

- Be respectful. We've seen countless requests come in that treat the gatekeeper with a dismissive attitude. Being disrespectful makes it easy for the gatekeeper to dismiss a request.

- Be informed about the influencer they represent. Integrate the knowledge you've gained about their brand into your outreach somehow. Mention how you enjoyed their book or recent blog post. Talk about how their content has helped you. Make it clear you've done your research.

- Gatekeepers are paid to protect their brand. The good ones can quickly determine if a request is worth their time, which is another reason to come to the conversation prepared. Since they are paid to protect the brand, you are challenged with convincing them they don't need to protect the brand from you.

- Keep in mind the fact that your request or outreach is likely one of dozens they will receive and review this week.

- Determine the value the gatekeeper and influencer would receive from interacting with you. Why should they consider your request above others coming their way?

- Be confident in who you are. Don't apologize for reaching out if you truly have something of value to bring to their attention.

- Don't let "no" deter your efforts. Your success is not defined by any one person or influencer deciding to work with you. Keep moving forward regardless.

We've recently had two perfect examples of what NOT to do when reaching out to a brand. One came via email within the last few months and another came via text message just a few days ago … so it's fresh in my (David's) mind.

1. *The email(s!)*

We represent several authors and experts and our team is considered the gatekeeper for those influencers. An email came in from someone wanting an endorsement from one of our highest-profile authors. The person reaching out had a book nearing completion and they wanted to attach the name and credibility of our author to their project in order to help secure a traditional publishing deal.

The person sent not one, not two, but three consecutive emails to me. Each seemingly longer than the last. In total, the word count between those three emails was over 3,000. Each one talked about how great he is and how amazing his story was, and how if he only had our endorsement, then the publishing world and readers everywhere would finally benefit from what he had to say.

Everything in those emails was about him. About his book. About how great he is and how everyone else was missing out because he was unknown. There were several references to how no one would give him a chance, and how he deserved to have more recognition than what he was currently experiencing. His lack of success was the fault of everyone else refusing to help him. The emails were all about him, and they went on and on.

There was no mention of me or of the author we represent. There was no mention of the work our author is currently doing or how our author might be connected to the content of the book he wanted endorsed.

There was zero value for our author or our company in this outreach, so my decision was immediate. We would decline the request and move on. This might sound harsh, but the reality is you will be dismissed instantly, like we did in this situation, if you make your outreach all about you. Self-centered people aren't usually endearing. But you aren't self-centered, right? Instead, you actively choose to be endearing in your outreach, right? Good. Glad we are on the same page about that! :-)

The man wanting the endorsement was (unsurprisingly) upset at my decision, and he shared his anger with us in a final email … an email that was even more off-putting than the first three. I was sad to see someone handle themselves in such a manner, but in another sense, that last email confirmed exactly what we'd been thinking to that point. It cemented the fact that we made the right decision to pass on the request.

Had this person taken the time to send an email containing anything of value for our author or our company, at the very least the outcome would have been a friendly exchange and a new relationship being created. We likely wouldn't have endorsed his book either way, but there could've been future opportunities to consider. But he chose to be aggressive, dismissive, selfish, rude, and uniformed. So it's unlikely we will consider any future requests.

If you find yourself in a situation where you've done all you can to endear yourself to your target influencer and they still say "no," just tell yourself that it's going to be OK. Don't send anything in writing today that you'll regret tomorrow. Don't go scorched-earth just because you didn't get what you wanted. This isn't a daycare for three-year-olds. Be OK with hearing "no." If it helps your mind, pretend that person is saying "not now" instead of "no." Put them on your list to reach out to again in six months. Keep exchanges friendly and full of gratitude if at all possible.

2. *The text message:*

A radio host recently texted one of our authors directly. The number came in as "unknown," but the phrasing in the text caused our author to pause. The text said:

"Hi. (Host's name redacted) here. Radio guy. I am on a new station... Would you mind to do an interview? It could include...your latest book? Thanks. God Bless..."

I've taken out some pieces of the text that weren't relevant, but you get the idea. This is clearly a mass text that was sent to several different interview targets, and the text included absolutely nothing personal about the recipient.

Opening with nothing more than "Hi." told us all we needed to know. The text was all about the texter. Nothing in the text had anything included about our author. No mention of our author's name or most recent book by its title. No mention of anything our author has been doing online or of the content he's been producing over the past several years. Nothing of value to our author at all.

The texter's approach is all about him. It looks and feels like spam. It's self-centered, riddled with confusing phrasing and punctuation, and not at all on par with the standard radio interview request we receive from noteworthy stations. It stands out in all the wrong ways.

Our author forwarded the text to me and asked me to look into the person. Of course, we said we would, but we already had all the info we needed even before doing the research.

Looking into the texter continued to prove out what we already knew—this was not something for us to pursue. Everything the texter did and said was all about him. This is not the right way to build relationships and approach influencers.

To top it all off, in our research, we found a recent tweet that confirmed every suspicion and concern I'd had up to that point. In this tweet, the texter was calling out and hashtagging another notable personality, who up to that point, had not responded to the interview requests of the texter. The texter didn't get the interview he wanted so instead of being a professional adult, he went to Twitter and called out his target … he tweeted at the target, tagged family members of the target, and hashtagged several questionable phrases, all in an effort to get this person to agree to doing a radio interview. This guy believed his aggressive approach was helping him. It would be a funny situation to me if it wasn't so sad. And maybe if we didn't see this kind of thing so often. This person actually believed that publicly shaming his target was going to make the interview more likely to happen. So bizarre. So unnecessary.

So many mistakes were made by this person and each one of them is easily avoidable for you. When reaching out to influencers, start with the assumption that they don't need you. They *might* benefit from engaging with you, but assume they are fine without you. The challenge for you is to determine why that person should care that you are reaching out to them.

In this situation when reaching out to influencers (and even on a bigger scale when writing your book in general), it's not about you.

Read those words again—it's not about you.

Ouch, right? But think about it. The entire point of you writing a book isn't about you, correct? You wrote something in order to influence or help others. So it's not about you. Instead, it's about the people who will be impacted by what you wrote. It's about the reader.

So keep that in mind when you are creating your marketing strategy. When it comes to reaching out to influencers, it's about the recipient. It's about the influencer. It's about the person you are contacting. What is the value they are going to receive from communicating with you? What is their takeaway? Why should they consider responding to you? Why should they say yes to whatever it is you are asking them to do?

If you have a personal relationship with an influencer, then it's fine to ask for a favor. Favors can be about you. That's OK. But when you are reaching out to someone you have no previous connection to or relationship with, the default position in your mind should be "What is in it for THEM?"

Take this humble approach and your interactions with influencer targets will have the best chance of success.

Who to approach and how to find them

Now that you understand how to approach influencers, you're ready to start making a target list of influencers to reach out to. There are a multitude of ways to get started, but let's begin by just taking a beat and setting expectations.

You're going to hear no. And you're going to hear it a lot.

Influencers are busy people, and even with the best approach, you're going to run into influencers who can't help, or just don't want to. Don't let that keep you from pursuing. Outreach at its core, is a numbers game.

And another note: Don't let the "no" color your perception of the person you're reaching out to. Remember that one day, you'd like to be where they are. Consider what it would feel like to deal with hundreds of requests each year from people who simply want you to say yes. Would saying yes help you reach your brand's purpose? Likely not. Instead, it can be a distraction. Keep the perspective of the previous section close at hand:

It's not about you.

With that mindset, here's how we'd get started researching who to reach out to:

Build a list of 100 people for your initial outreach. You'll set up an Excel spreadsheet or Google Sheet with the following columns:

- Website
- Domain rating
- Contact info
- Guest post guidelines
- Post you liked

Depending on your niche, this can be as simple as typing the following prompt into Google:

Best [podcast/blog/radio show/etc] on [niche topic]

So, for instance, if we were releasing an author marketing book, we might search on Google for the best blogs on writing. This search alone will give us thousands of results, but we're looking for one type of blog post in particular—the listicle.

On the listicle post, you'll have 10-30 different blogs on the topic you're looking for. Most of these posts also link to the media. So, open each of those links in a new tab.

Then, start to fill in the columns on your spreadsheet.

The first column (website) is obvious, just copy and paste the website URL into the spreadsheet.

Then, for domain rating, use a tool like AHREFs to search out this number. Here's the link:

https://ahrefs.com/website-authority-checker

ASIDE on domain rating: This is a good stat to know, but it's not a be-all, end-all stat. Domain rating ranks websites based on their viewed authority of Google. It's a proprietary formula that AHREFs has come up with to help you understand the impact a guest post might have if it's on a particular website. So, we will use this as a sorting mechanism a bit later, but for now, you can just put that number in the column.

Now, if you're going to reach out to a particular website, you need a contact there. There are a couple of ways to find this. One is to search the website and then add mailto: in Google. As an example, for Jerry's site, you could search:

Jerryjenkins.com "mailto:"

That would return all the email addresses on the site.

The other way is to scour the site yourself and look for the contact information. A lot of sites will list email addresses like this:

Firstname [at] website [dot] com

That prevents non-humans from finding the contact email. Luckily, as a human, looking carefully through the site gives you an advantage over the machines.

Next, search for guest post guidelines on the site. This will help you if you are interested to know exactly what kind of post the website is looking for. There's a ton of opportunity to get this wrong, and your attention to detail makes it more likely that when you get a yes, you actually get published on the site.

Finally, as you're researching the website, go ahead and make a note of a particular post you liked. This will help make your outreach personal—again, read human.

Before you start reaching out, sort your list. Domain rating is a great first filter to sort with. As you're reaching out, we'd suggest starting at the bottom of the list and working your way up. That way, your first outreach attempts can be used as a way to validate the template and test to see what type of outreach works best.

Once you've finished these steps, you're ready for outreach.

Here's a template that we've used with some success over the years:

SUBJECT: Quick Question
BODY:

Hey [first name]!

I was doing some research on blogs in the [niche topic] space, and yours came to the top of my list. I love the blog, especially the post on [post topic].

I know you [usually do/don't] accept guest posts, but I have a book coming out on the topic, and I'd love to provide your readers with some valuable content.

Here are a few topics that I thought may be interesting to your folks based on my research:

[TOPIC 1]
[TOPIC 2]

[TOPIC 3]

If you're interested, I'd love to send you a first draft. If not, no worries, I'll keep following along as a fan of your work.

Talk soon!
[your name]

A couple of notes about templates:

1. There are so many ways to mess this up, so the key to a good template is a good editor. Make sure to double check every field you're filling in.

2. Even a good template may only work 3-5 percent of the time. That's OK. Keep tweaking until you get to these percentages.

3. Once you've had some successful guest posts, add them in here as social proof.

I (Chase) didn't want to tell this story, but I feel like I have to ... One time, it was my job to be in charge of the outreach emails. I was using a mail app that had several different inboxes and outboxes of mine attached to it. This meant that all of my work email accounts and all of my personal email accounts were right there in the same place. All right next to each other. So convenient! What could go wrong? Well, the worst thing that could have happened did: I sent a large outreach email to a large group of influencer targets from my personal AOL email address from 1999. Do you recall how people chose email addresses with AOL in the 90's? It was based on whatever you were doing in life at that time. Let's just say my

AOL email address was … embarrassing. And every single one of our target influencers at the time would agree! Ugh.

But it wasn't all bad. We got a yes anyway from one of our top targets.

So, be careful to double check each aspect of the template, but also remember that the mistakes are going to happen. Embrace them. Grieve them. And then, ten years later, laugh about them and write about them in a book. It's all part of the process.

This is a tedious process, but it's worthwhile. If you can borrow other people's audiences to build your own platform, it's more likely that you'll have a successful book launch.

So, put in the time, and make sure you're providing tremendous value along the way.

CHAPTER 13:

Cover Design and Book Layout

Did you know that we can spot a self-published book a mile away?

Literally.

OK, not literally—but figuratively, we can. Because most self-published books don't take into account this chapter.

If you're publishing with a traditional publisher, you'll have input in this process, but at the end of the day, it's usually their decision what the design and layout of the book looks like. They have professionals on staff who do this all day every day. They bring design ideas to the table so you don't have to. You can give feedback and share your opinions, but you are likely working from a variety of options, all of which are industry accepted and high quality.

But going the self-published route is different. As a self-published author, you take the reins on this and every other portion of the book publishing process. This is another part of the self- publishing process that is crucial though, so here are some tips on how to design a cover like a pro, and how to make sure your book layout fools even the best eagle eye.

When you're designing a book cover, it's easy to jump into one of those apps that helps you edit things (like Canva) and create something that you think looks great, but there are a few steps that you need to take to make sure that the cover you come out with looks good enough.

1. Research your genre: You can go on Amazon and look at the top-selling books in your genre for your planned release. Take

note of the font, the pictures, the style. Take note of how the author's name is listed.

It's easy to make mistakes like putting "by" before the author name, but you'll quickly notice that traditionally published books don't do that. It's also easy to use a script font that makes the title or author's name hard to read, but you'll notice the traditionally published books don't do that either.

Try to match the style of your book cover to the style of the genre. And give it something to stand out. Mimic success, but add your own unique twist.

Look at twenty-five other books in your genre that have been traditionally published in the last ten years and make note of what each of those covers include and what they don't include. Become familiar with what is commonly used and what is never used. Don't make the mistake of assuming your book cover doesn't matter. We realize that asking you to do research like this is one just more thing to add to your plate, but it is important. Don't skip important steps!

2. Design for the thumbnail: We mentioned briefly the script font may make the title hard to read. If it's hard to read on your computer screen when you have the cover blown up to a large size, think how much harder it will be to read when the cover is a thumbnail on Goodreads or Amazon. Make it clear and punchy so that you could read it from a mile away.

3. Color: We are not going to pretend that we know anything about color theory, especially since about 90 percent of my shirts are

blue. Instead, just know that certain colors mean certain things. They communicate certain ideas. Be cognizant of that as you're designing your cover. Go back to your genre research and notice what colors are used most. Of those twenty-five books you are looking at in your genre, the odds are you'll find one or two colors that are used in half of those books. There is a reason for that being the case. The reason changes with each genre and audience, but the point is that you don't need to reinvent the color wheel. Study what is working already and figure out a way to make it work for you.

4. Bring in the middle schooler: This sounds like dumb advice, but when you're designing a book cover, sometimes you miss the most obvious things because you're too close to the process. This is when we encourage you to bring in the middle schooler. And yes, I (Chase) have stories to tell you what I mean:

When I was young, my mother was in charge of designing a brochure for an event called Ladies' First Thursday. The apostrophe placement in that brochure was challenging enough, but when she received 1000 brochures printed with the title: Ladies' First Thrusday, the only person who caught the mistake was my sister—a middle schooler at the time.

And here's the example of why it needs to be a middle schooler: A while ago, I was in the design process for a prominent author whose book was coming out and the thumbnail was going up on Amazon. The book title might've made an immature middle schooler chuckle, but what made it a slam dunk was the symbol on the front cover that had a phallic resemblance. Not everyone would've made the connection to that symbol, but once someone said it out loud, our entire team saw it and agreed that a change needed to happen. We needed the middle schooler in the room to call those things out in order for the cover to go in a different direction. Can you imagine if the middle schooler hadn't said anything? (Spoiler: Sometimes you have to be the middle-schooler.)

5. When in doubt, ask a professional. At the end of the day, a cover is a crucial part of the buying process for your target audience. You always hear the phrase, "don't judge a book by its cover." Let me tell you—that's not how this industry works. I remember going to a book awards ceremony and chuckling at the irony of the fact that the first award was for the most creative cover design. Literally, at the largest award show for the industry, all the professionals were judging books by their cover. So that old cliche phrase holds true for everything except the thing it is actually describing. Book covers are judged by every single reader. If yours is not resonating with your target audience, then it won't matter how great your book is because that reader will never make it past the cover.

All that is to say: you need to get the cover right. If you don't have a design eye, find someone who does. A lot of times you can find the book cover designer listed on the Copyright Notification Page of other books. Don't hesitate to look up the designers of your favorite covers and see what they would charge to design your book cover. The worst that can happen is either they say "no" or that you can't afford to hire them to help. Either way, if you don't have any clue how to attack this cover design process, it is worth your time to reach out and ask someone who knows.

Speaking of copyright notification pages…let's talk a bit about book layout.

One of the easiest ways to spot a self-published book is that they have the internal layout of their book wrong.

There are a ton of different ways this can rear its head: margins, acknowledgements in the wrong place, font choice, and so on. But there are enough resources out there to get book layouts professionally done that you don't have to make this mistake.

Have a copyright notification page. This is always at the front of the book.

Have acknowledgements. Depending on the genre, these can be at the front or the back. In general, we recommend acknowledgements be at the back of the book. The reasoning behind that suggestion is that you want a little distraction for the reader as possible before they get into actually reading your book.

Have a dedication. This is almost always at the front of a book. The reason a dedication is fine at the front but that acknowledgements aren't is usually because the dedication is extremely short. Regarding a dedication, Jerry Jenkins says the following:

(The dedication page is where) you tell who the book is to.

Maybe a loved one or a favorite mentor. Keep it short.

It will mean the most to the person in question, so don't bore readers with a paragraph

about something personal.

To Sherry; she knows why.

Something like this is plenty. It can certainly be longer if needed, but your goal as the author should be to keep the dedication as short as possible.

Get some endorsements. You've put in the time and effort to write your book, but now you need to have someone else attach their name and/or their support of what you've written. Make a list of potential people in your life who you could reach out to for an endorsement. This list should include other authors in your genre, influencers you admire, experts in your field, and people in your life who hold any kind of notable position or professional title. This is another area where you are likely to receive many "no" responses, but if you have a list of people to target, your odds of getting a few positive replies will increase. Don't be afraid to send out a lot of endorsement requests. Some people who are interested in giving an endorsement will ask to see the entire manuscript and that is fine. Most of the time when you are seeking endorsements, you want people to give a statement of approval of your writing. To do so, they'll need to read some or all of your manuscript and then give you their endorsement. Just make sure you are clear in those situations that the document you are sending (the document containing the manuscript) is confidential, unpublished, and should not be shared with anyone else.

In some cases, specifically those dealing with people who are in your immediate social circles, they might prefer to provide an endorsement of you as an author in general rather than a specific endorsement of the manuscript in question. They might say something like, "(Your Name) has a wonderful gift for weaving practical principles into a captivating story." This kind of endorsement is still useful for you even if it doesn't speak directly to or about the book you've written. Any kind of endorsement you can acquire, whether it's from another author or a respected friend, can be useful in your efforts.

The point of making sure each of these four sections are included in your book is to help your book look and feel like a traditionally published book, even if it is self-published. Because we can tell you that if it doesn't, you'll be hard pressed to get the attention of the people you are trying to reach. They simply don't have time for projects that don't pay attention to detail. It would be a shame for them to miss out on your writing simply because you failed to include some of these key elements.

Take note of the layout of the books in your genre. Try to emulate them, and if you can't, find a professional with experience in doing book layouts to help you. Again, don't skip steps.

PART IV

Drafting a Marketing Plan

If we were you at this point, we'd be thinking something like:

Remind me again why I'm the one drafting a marketing plan? I'm the author. I didn't sign up for this. I just wanted to write a book.

Let us remind you of a couple of things by giving you a peek behind the curtain of the publishing industry.

Publishing companies publish hundreds of books per year. Some of the larger companies publish thousands. As if that weren't enough competition, self-publishing has brought an additional deluge of new works into the market. Conservatively, there are thousands of self-published books released every day. That's well over one million books hitting the market each year, and some studies say it's actually closer to two million than it is to one million. Think about that … it means every single day, there are 3,000-4,000 new books being published. Amazing!

When faced with those staggering numbers, an author that we worked with decided to build an internal team to market his books. Not because the publishing company wasn't doing their own marketing campaigns. Instead, he built his own team because he knew that no one would care more about the books he was publishing in any given year than he would. The author knew he could have the best agent or publisher in the world, but that those people and their staff of experts would still not have as much focus or passion for his books that he would.

His perspective was something like this: *I'll sell the rights of my book to the publishing company so they can print and distribute my book. The publisher is infinitely better positioned to print and distribute than I am, so I will let them do what they are great at doing. But for everything else, I want to control whatever it is that I can control. I'll still handle the marketing of the book. I'll handle the grassroots efforts. Anything the publisher can add in my areas of influence will be considered icing on the cake, but I'm going to control what I can control.*

Specifically, through his efforts—and in combination with the efforts of the publishing company— he had a book hit the *New York Times* bestseller list six months <u>after</u> its initial release.

You may not know how odd that statement is. Most books are marketed in such a way that they are slated for release with a big marketing push. Then, the publishing company will let the market determine what to do next. If the book takes off, the publishing company will put more marketing dollars behind it. If the book doesn't perform well, the publishing company will move on to the next book launch. They're in the volume business.

Here, the author knew that his book was the only one he would write that year, so after the initial marketing push from him and the publishing company didn't perform to expectations, he got to work while the publishing company moved on. He pushed to get the book into as many hands as possible. Six months later, the book appeared on a morning talk show on television, and the rest is history. It hit the *New York Times* Bestsellers list and has since sold well over a million copies, and has been translated into over thirty languages around the world. It's an astounding story of perseverance. The author did not allow the slow initial sales to deter him from continuing to do everything in his power to get the book into the hands of more people.

This story is not to discourage you—not in the least! This story should to encourage you. Like the author in the story, no one will care as much about your book release as you do. So, build a plan—a plan you can implement—to market your book so that when it launches, it has a ready-made group of buyers waiting for the release. And if the buyers aren't there quite yet, add marketing initiatives for post launch pushes. This will separate you from the pack of those authors who are relying on the publishing company to print, distribute, market, and sell their work.

And with the odds we listed earlier (thousands of new books releasing every day!), why wouldn't you do everything you can to make your book a success?

We've talked about it before, but it is worth repeating. There are many parts to this author marketing process that have nothing to do with your actual writing ability. Sadly, not everything is based on the quality of your book. We all wish that wasn't the case but because it's true, determine now to create a plan for how to deal with that reality.

The reality, of course, is that you have to figure out a way for your book to stand out from the other one million books being released in the next twelve months. It's a daunting task to take on, but for you to find success as an author, you need to be willing to face the challenge. The following chapters will help you do exactly that!

CHAPTER 14:

Choosing Your Channels

You have an amazing manuscript that you think will change the way the world reads. Your name will constantly be on the minds of your readers, but you don't know where to start in marketing the book.

The answer? You start by identifying key marketing channels. On these channels, you'll make noise about your book launch, provide immense value to your target audience, and hopefully, sell more than a few copies of your book.

Still, one of the biggest obstacles that authors face is choosing the right marketing channels for their book launch strategy. So, let's talk through what a marketing channel is, and then, we will talk through how to choose the best channel for your book.

A marketing channel is simply an avenue where target audiences and products meet. In your case, a marketing channel is where your target audience will find out about your book.

Need a few examples?

Here are a couple that we've used in the past to market books:

- Author website (remember why we had you set this up?)

- Author email list

- Author social media pages
    - Facebook
    - TikTok

- Instagram
- Pinterest, etc.
- Target audience genre-specific communities
  - Book clubs
  - Facebook groups
  - Groupme chats
  - Mastermind groups
  - Conferences, especially in the case of nonfiction
  - Social clubs
  - Forums
- Media outlets
  - Magazines
  - Radio stations
  - Podcasts
  - YouTube channels
  - Television channels
- Influencers for Target Audience
- Paid advertisements
  - Social ads
  - Search engine ads
  - Traditional media Ads
- Brand partnerships

As you're looking through this list, you might get overwhelmed, so take some encouragement from these wise words:

Don't judge a person until you walk a mile in their shoes.

In this instance, it means you need to walk a mile in your target audience's shoes in order to determine where they are the most likely to be found. Once you've done that, decide which marketing channels make the most sense to pursue in order to reach more of those people.

If you're after a young and upcoming group, for instance, you're not going to spend all your marketing dollars on targeted Facebook ads. Your audience likely doesn't hang out there. You might look to TikTok or Instagram, or whatever the new social media platform of the day is.

You've got to make the decision that you're going to fish where the fish are.

You might think that this is referring to those secret spots that fishermen hide from each other where they believe the best fish are to be found. You know, the ones they pass down to the next generation as if it was an inheritance. Let's be clear: that's not at all what I'm talking about.

When we say, "Fish where the fish are," we mean you need to find where they are stocking the fish into the lake, get to that spot, set up camp, and wait there for a mountain of fish to catch. If you know where your target audience is, where they hang out, how they behave, then it becomes a lot easier to engage with them. It becomes much easier to cast your line when you know the fish are already sitting there.

Marketing expert Ramit Sethi tells the story of his father taking him fishing. It goes something like this:

One day, my dad woke me up and said,

"Do you want to go fishing today,"

I knew it was going to be a hilarious day.

So, we go fishing – there was a fish hatchery close to our house, and it turned out that day, they were releasing millions of fish into the lake. So, we sit there, and put our pole out and we're catching nothing—it's been thirty minutes, sixty minutes ... nothing.

We're kind of getting bored and starting to complain to our dad, and our dad looks at us with a gleam in his eye, and he said, "Come with me."

So, he walked us over to the actual pipe where thousands of fish every minute are coming out. So, we put our pole there, and we catch, like, 20 fish in 30 seconds…

…what I learned from that day:

1. *My dad is a horrible fisherman*

2. *It got a lot more fun when I went where the fish are*

In marketing, it's the same—you go where the fish are. Don't try to use a marketing channel because it's the next up and coming thing, or because you've heard about it and you feel pressured into participating. Instead, use the channel that best fits the target audience you're trying to reach. We'll talk more about this concept later, but for now, keep this story in your mind and use it as a guideline when you're identifying marketing channels.

Walk a mile in your target audience's shoes. Revisit the empathy map you worked on in Part I. Based on their answers to those questions, where does your target audience hang out the most?

Once you've done that, you can start moving through the other steps in this section and building out a marketing plan.

One of the best places to start?

Dive into competitor research for other books written in your genre.

CHAPTER 15:

Competitor Research

Authors often feel like (and we've mentioned this throughout this book) that their message is innovative, even revolutionary, and so it applies to everyone. There is no niche. There are no competitors. The marketing strategy doesn't exist because nothing like their book has ever been written before.

When we hear this from authors, we're often reminded of the wise words of Solomon in Ecclesiastes:

What has been will be again, what has been done will be done again; there is nothing new under the sun.

Books are not a place to innovate—at least not from a genre perspective. You need to understand where in the lay of the landscape your book fits so that you can find the largest group possible to market your book to.

This may seem counterintuitive. So, let me explain by using an example. Recently, we were thinking through the book series by Suzanne Collins, *The Hunger Games*. (And yes, sometimes we sit and think about why a particular book series found success. It's not weird if you get paid to do it, right?) You may know it—the premise is that there's a terrible lottery where children from twelve districts are chosen to compete in a to-the-death style competition. Whoever wins, wins forever acclaim. Whoever loses dies.

As we were considering the work, we thought to ourselves that the premise was interesting but not new. The premise reminded us of the short story, *The Lottery*, by Shirley Jackson. That story was printed in the New

Yorker in 1948. In it, a young woman wins the small town's lottery and her prize is being stoned to death.

But, we couldn't think of any other similar stories or novel length works that had a similar premise.

So, should there be a category of books for dystopian lotteries that end in death? Was Suzanne Collins aiming at that particular niche?

Let's check the record on Amazon:

The first book in the series falls into three categories:

- Children's Dystopian Fiction Books
- Teen & Young Adult Fiction about Self Esteem & Reliance
- Teen & Young Adult Science Fiction Action & Adventure

So, even with a unique novel-length premise, Suzanne found herself squarely in some huge genres that attract large numbers of readers. Even though her content was innovative and the writing was done in a unique way, the book itself was simply categorized.

How does this apply to what you're writing?

Have you looked recently at the number of categories on Amazon for books?

There are over 10,000 to choose from!

If you can't fit your message into one of those categories, you need to try again.

Why? Because when you do, you know that there's already some modicum of an audience for your book. Further, you can start doing competitor research to make sure that your book hits the musts of a genre and also fills the gaps within the genre that are missing.

You'll find out how customers are talking about books like yours, and you can start to use their own words to inform your marketing strategies.

This is now the second time we've talked about mining reviews. You may be asking: how do you mine reviews? It's easier than it sounds:

1. Click through Amazon to the category that your book will ultimately be published under

2. Find the bestselling books in the category

3. Start to read the reviews of customers (both positive and negative)

You'll then use these to create key takeaways as you're drafting your book.

Second, you'll use the titles of the books for competitive research.

Specifically, take the titles, and search for them in Google. Then, determine how they marketed the book by keeping a keen eye on:

1. What interviews they did (and with which publications)

2. Where they have active social media presences (you need to look at both the author and the book)

3. Do an image search to see if you can identify any ads that were run when the book was launched. Then, look and see where those ads were placed.

4. What themes did the book hit on, and how does your book hit on those themes in a different or unique way?

You need to be a detective. Find what worked and what didn't work for your competition, so that you can distinguish your work from theirs.

As an example, here's a recent review mining that we did for an author writing in the Christian historical fiction genre. As she was preparing to write her book length work, she was thinking through the different types of categories that her book could fall into, but she didn't know where to start. We stepped in by identifying the target customer, finding the category that customer would read books from, and then reading the reviews to see what that audience loved, what they missed, and how the author could meet those needs in her work.

* * *

Target Customer Research Example:

The most important part of marketing isn't the offer, the price, or the reach. It's knowing exactly who you're talking to. Only then can you talk to that person how they *need* to be talked to in order to get them to purchase.

In this Target Market Research, a great deal of effort goes into discovering what your target customer is like. So, we have zeroed in on your likely best "Hypothetical Reader."

In our research to find your reader, we studied Amazon reviews in these categories:

- Historical Fiction
- Christian Historical Fiction
- Religious Historical Fiction

Below, you'll see a few of the key reviews that we believe embody your target reader:

"In my opinion, most religious fiction is not very good as everyone is just too nice or the scenes just aren't realistic as it's not "Christian" to write about how people really are. Lynn Austin, on the other hand, does a really nice job of fictionalizing a brief passage of the Bible into a full-length novel, and gets you into the heads of the characters. The imagery and scenery are very realistic and, for example, I could imagine me walking the dusty streets of the Middle Ages. The thing that struck me the most was this book really got me thinking and getting more out of the story than a random section of the 28th chapter of the book of Second Chronicles and makes me want to read the next one in the series: with the volume of books I read on a monthly basis, having one stick with me and recalling various sections of the book long after I read it (about a month ago) is, to me, impressive and tells me this was really a good book."

- 5-star rating from Gods and Kings (Chronicles of the Kings #1) (Volume 1)

- **Takeaway: This audience wants to be pulled into the history, to feel it and sense it as if they were walking around in it.**

Oftentimes reading the Old Testament it is hard to piece everything together. Lynn Austin does a fantastic job of weaving the biblical text from the account of the kings and the prophets along with Jewish traditions that bring it to life.

My only complaint would be her use of Yahweh. I understand her reasoning to differentiate the One True God from all the other gods, but for Orthodox Jews that is a sacred name of God. It was the very personal name of God given to Moses (translated as I AM in most English versions of the Bible). Jews only spoke that name 1 time a year during Yom Kippur and even then only by the high priest while praying in the Temple in the Holiest of Holies. I wish she had chosen from El ("God"), Eloah ("God"), Elohim ("Gods"), Shaddai ("God Almighty"), Ehyeh, and Tzevaot ("[of] Hosts") instead to refer to God.

- 5-star rating from Gods and Kings (Chronicles of the Kings #1) (Volume 1)

- **Takeaway: This audience is often very knowledgeable about the history around what they're reading, which is why they started reading this book in the first place. They want to increase that knowledge. This is their pet subject to learn more about. Therefore, you need to have a high standard of excellence in your research to get them into it.**

Whatever the explanation, I could not get into this story. The characters lacked depth (albeit not distinct characteristics), the language was jarringly time-period inappropriate (which didn't bother me in other books, maybe because I got so thoroughly sucked in to the story?), and I found the process of reading this book to be a task, rather than a pleasure.

- 1-star rating from Gods and Kings (Chronicles of the Kings #1) (Volume 1)

- **Takeaway: A significant portion of this audience would be disappointed if everything wasn't time-period appropriate.**

I think Tessa Afshar handled the story brilliantly. Not only did she weave us a beautiful and entertaining tapestry, but she also addressed the deeper journey—that of redemption from a life of sin. God took a terribly flawed heart and filled it with love. This book showed me how God meets us at whatever place on the road we've walked to. And He does it with all of us. The good, the bad, and the ugly inside.

Pearl in the Sand did this without belaboring the points. I really felt a kinship with Rahab and with her friend Miriam. I agonized with her over the difficulty of talking to those we feel have wronged us in the past—of how important it is to forgive them, so that we can also receive forgiveness.

- 5-star rating from *Pearl in the Sand*

- **Takeaway: Within these old stories, people are looking for new ways they can relate to the ancient characters in their modern life.**

However a few things grated on me, and I finally had to just quit reading. One thing was the heroine's thoughts about theology. They just didn't have the right feel for the time period . . . These thoughts were just too related to Christian doctrine to feel right for the earliest days of the Hebrews.

- 3-star rating from *Pearl in the Sand*

- **Takeaway: Getting the research right—and making sure it determines the feel of the story—is important to a significant portion of this audience.**

The novel reads like an old mythic tale, told with simple descriptive prose, and playful dialogue: the characters even refer to themselves in the third person! While reading Siddhartha, I couldn't help but picture the novel's world as being hand drawn, like the old drawings of the Buddha and the Hindu and Buddhist mythologies of old.

- 5-star rating from *Siddhartha*

- **Takeaway: Less religious history buffs often want to be engrossed in the wonder of old religions, and this could be their entry point into your book.**

Hermann Hesse's Siddhartha is an absolutely amazing and engrossing tale of one man's journey to find that all-elusive idea of enlightenment. The book's title may suggest that it is simply a story that would have value only for people of the Buddhist persuasion, but this simply is not true. The work is well written and thought out, and it does a terrific job of showing us as human beings that oftentimes what we are looking for is with us all along.

- 5-star rating from *Siddhartha*

- **Takeaway: Searchers are looking for wisdom within religious books, regardless of the religion.**

America's First Daughter brings a turbulent era to vivid life. All the conflicts and complexities of the Early Republic are mirrored in Patsy's story. It's breathlessly exciting and heartbreaking by turns-a personal and political page-turner.

- Review of *America's First Daughter* by Donna Thorland, author of *The Turncoat*

- **Takeaway: This audience wants to be engrossed in the era in which they're reading. It looks like they often choose an era**

that intrigues them, and read within that era.

I have read numerous books on Thomas Jefferson and know the history of the Revolution and the French Revolution fairly well. I was looking forward to reading about the President's daughter, although I knew a little prior to reading. I felt the undocumented romance between "Patsy" and William short did not add anything, yet it took up almost the first half of the book, then jumped quickly to her marriage to Thomas Mann Randolph. The Randolphs and Jeffersons were related, but this didn't seem to really come through in the book. If this had been my first encounter with Thomas Jefferson I would have come away with a very disappointed view of the man. Never did I really get an idea of the "great" sacrifices he made for this country, nor any evidence of his brilliance. As for the daughter, I don't seem to have a feeling for her one way or another, certainly not one of great respect, which I thought I would have after reading the book. Disappointed in the history content and in the way the life of Patsy Jefferson Randolph was developed.

- 1-star review of *America's First Daughter*

- **Takeaway: If someone feels like the history paints an inaccurate depiction of a historical character they care about, this audience won't enjoy it.**

Here is the suggested avatar you should chase at the beginning of the your journey:

Customer Avatar: "Historical Hannah"

* * *

Hopefully, from this example, you can see the depth of research that can (and should) go into this competitive research. And this is only the first step! Remember after gathering this information, the author needs to go to Google and search the book titles to gather even more information about the genre and her place within it.

The good news? Most of the authors that we know love this type of research. It's one of the marketing tasks that you can be great at, because you also have to do this kind of research for the content of your book.

So, take time. Understand that there's no singular right way to accomplish this, and have fun with the process.

BONUS Note: If you want to have a little extra fun, read some of the 1-star reviews on the greatest novels of all time. It's a hoot! Here's a good one from one of our favorite books, *To Kill a Mockingbird*:

Review Title: *Way below expectations*

Reviewed in the United States on June 9, 2021

Verified Purchase

I think the story gist is in 1% of the book, the rest of the story I found it boring.

CHAPTER 16:

Marketing Initiatives

Now that you've chosen your marketing channels, and you've plunged yourself deep into the competitive research for your genre, you're ready to start brainstorming some marketing initiatives.

There are literally thousands of ways to market your book, and you need to choose the right ones to give your book the greatest chance of success.

One time, we were having a staff retreat, and the goal was to come up with a board full of marketing initiatives for a particular project. We sat at that board for hours, as people threw hundreds of ideas back and forth. Eventually, the board was completely full of implementable marketing initiatives. Of course, thinking back on it, the sky writing idea did seem a bit far-fetched...

But, you need to have fun with this process. So, to help you view this as a fun exercise, we suggest viewing marketing initiatives as tests— experiments to determine what will and what won't work to move the needle in your book marketing process. We will discuss this mindset more later, but just to give you a foundation, we need to talk a little bit about the Pareto Principle:

In 1906, an Italian economist named Vilfredo Pareto created a mathematical formula to describe the unequal division of wealth in his country. The Pareto principle (also known as the 80/20 rule or the law of the vital few) states that in many cases, roughly 80 percent of the effects of action comes from 20 percent of the causes. Pareto showed that approximately 80 percent of the land and wealth in Italy was owned by 20 percent of the population.

Here's how this applies to your marketing efforts: Of all of the tests you run, 20 percent of those will produce 80 percent of the results. That means that your job in this instance is two-fold:

1. You have to run a bunch of tests

2. When you identify the Pareto Principle taking effect, double down on what's working

So many times in the book creation process, authors get bogged down by failure. Let me be straight with you: Failure is going to happen in this process.

You will fail to hit deadlines

You will fail to hit sales goals

You will fail to reach the market you intended

You may even fail to get published

Regardless of all of these, however, your success is completely dependent on your ability to treat failure as learning. Then, take that learning and figure out the "figure-out-able"—who *will* buy your book, and how you can reach them.

So, write down some marketing initiatives, and if you're struggling to get some in place, here's a brief list of different categories to try to brainstorm within:

Pie-in-the-sky options

Examples:

- Get chosen for Reese Witherspoon's book club

- Be featured on *Good Morning America*

- Have Jerry Jenkins (or your favorite influencer) post on Facebook about my book

- Hook a banner up to an airplane at my favorite beach

Expensive, but realistic options

Examples:

- Outsource
    - Hire a PR firm
    - Hire a book marketing agency
- Do it Yourself
    - Have organizations buy bulk copies of my books
    - Buy bulk copies of my books to sell at events
    - Pay for media to sell copies of my book (Facebook Ads, Google Ads, TV ads, etc.)

Groundswell options:

Examples:

- Ask if I can send free PDFs to influencers

- Send free PDFs to my friends to read

- Ask for reviews

- Post on my social media

- Reach out to blogs and podcasts to be interviewed on them

- Get on local television

- Be featured in my city's business journal

- Post a blog series about my book topic on my website

- Launch my book to my email list using a digital marketing formula

None of these options are easy, but as you can tell, there are varying levels of options available, and each option comes with its own challenges.

So, the big takeaway is this: brainstorm a ton of options. A brainstorm like this is much like the first draft of your book—you don't evaluate the brainstorm until you've exhausted your ideas. (Otherwise, you wouldn't even get to the sky writing idea.) Once you've listed all the ideas you can think of, then, after you've brainstormed, choose the most realistic and achievable options and set a goal to achieve them.

Once you've started to complete these goals and implement the marketing plan, be sure to measure the results to see where the Pareto Principle is taking effect. Double down on what's working and then ditch what's not working in favor of a new test.

CHAPTER 17:

SMART Goals

If you're anything like me (Chase), you sometimes set ambitious goals, and then you forget about the plans that you made? Does that sound familiar?

Let me give you an example. When I was a second grader, I had my eye on a particular young lady. And so I made a plan. I was going to be a vet, go to the college where her dad had gone, and we were going to be together forever.

She was never told that plan. And honestly, I forgot about it until I was writing this today, and was looking for an example of how I had made a plan that later failed.

(I didn't have to think for too long, by the way—this just happened to be the least embarrassing of my grandiose failures.)

Still, when you're planning marketing initiatives like we started to do above, it's crucial that you have a particular action plan in place to achieve the goals.

Why? Honestly, because it's science.

Check this out from Psychology Today:

There exists a wealth of research in the area of goal setting, particularly within organizational settings. Initially, this exploration began with the objective of ascertaining how the level of intended achievement (the goal) is related to the actual level of achievement (the performance) in an organizational setting (Locke, 1990).

The setting of goals has been shown to increase employee motivation and organizational commitment (Latham, 2004). Additionally, goals affect the intensity of our actions and our emotions – the more difficult and valued a goal is, the more intense our efforts will be in order to attain it, and the more success we experience following achievement (Latham & Locke, 2006).

Through the experience of success and the positive emotions that accompany it, confidence and belief in our own abilities grow. Schunk (1985) found that participation in goal setting encourages a search for new strategies to aid success. Finding novel ways to utilize our skills and push our abilities increases task-relevant knowledge while enhancing self-efficacy and self-confidence.

So, if we know that goals are important to set, it makes sense to give ourselves a framework to set them. One of the bests that we've seen developed is by using SMART goals.

If you're not familiar with SMART goals, they were developed by George Doran, Arthur Miller, and James Cunningham in a 1981 article. SMART is an acronym that stands for:

S - Specific

M - Measurable

A - Attainable

R - Realistic

T - Timely

So, let's walk this through a bit with your potential selling of your book:

If you want to sell 100 copies of your book, then to make it a SMART goal, you need to phrase it like so:

I want to sell 100 copies of my book (specific and measurable) in the next ninety days (timely) by emailing my list of 10,000 people (attainable and realistic).

A goal set this specifically is much more likely to be attained because you know exactly what you have to do by when to be successful.

At Leverage, we try to make all our goals this specific. It's not so that we can judge people when they fail (because we often fall short of our goals). Instead, it's so we can grow our muscle memory in setting and hitting attainable goals—and if we fail, we can pinpoint where the failure occurred and how to make it successful in the future.

Speaking of evaluating, let's revisit my grandiose plan failure earlier. The goal was to become a vet and marry the girl of my second-grade dreams.

Why did this fail? Let's apply the SMART framework to see:

Was the goal specific? For a second-grader, yeah. I (Chase) am giving myself that.

Was it measurable? I suppose so, you either become a vet or not, right?

Was it attainable? Here's where we start to see an issue – this particular goal had a few factors outside of my control.

1. I didn't tell the young lady, so how would she have known?

2. I hadn't applied to or gotten into vet school—although the idea of a Doogie Howser type show for a young veterinarian should absolutely be made into a TV show

So, here we fail, but for fun—let's continue.

Was it realistic? Highly likely that it was *not* realistic.

Was it timely? No, I didn't have an outside edge on how long the goal would take. And if you asked me today, that's probably the singular reason why this goal never happened—I learned how long veterinarians have to go to school for, and at that point, I was out.

I know this exercise was tongue-in-cheek, but you can go through the same process as you're evaluating your marketing goals. So, take a few of the initiatives that you identified in the previous chapter and apply them to this SMART goal framework. Try to have four of them ready before you start reading the next chapter.

CHAPTER 18:

Implementing a Marketing Plan

Implementing a marketing plan takes more than a SMART goal. It takes something that runs deeper. You have to have a foundational understanding of why you're trying to achieve your marketing plan, or else at the first sign of failure, you may fall away.

At Leverage, the way that we ensure that we are tying marketing plans to our foundation is to explain why we do what we say we're going to do. The below is an excerpt from our core values explanation document:

CORE VALUE 4. High Expectation, Healthy tension

When Chase was about to get married, he asked his 94-year-old grandfather for some advice. His words, "Do what you say you're going to do."

It has served Chase in his professional career, but it has also become a rallying cry for the Leverage Leadership. Let's be people who stand behind what we say and accomplish the goals we set out to accomplish.

This is why we take deadlines seriously. It's why we are meticulous in setting goals. It's why we try to not overcommit or grow faster than we are ready to. We do what we say we're going to do. And that means saying no, especially when that might be in jeopardy.

Living out this value will inevitably lead to the occasional difficult conversation. If someone isn't meeting deadlines or isn't doing what they said they would do, it will be discussed.

We will hold the team to a standard of high expectations and healthy tension.

As you can see in this brief explanation, the implementation that our team is able to accomplish is tied specifically to a core belief held by one of the founders. Then, it's cemented by remembering that our ability to implement has been directly tied to the successes that we have had. The value also anticipates the conflict that will arise, and gives us a path to deal with it.

So, in your mind, or on a sheet of paper, take a moment to answer these questions regarding your marketing plan:

- Why are you implementing your marketing plan?

- What would it mean to your career if you were able to implement the plan?

- What would it mean to your career if you failed to implement the plan?

- Who needs your content the most?

- How will your content help those people reach their goals?

- How will it entertain them?

Did you take the time to really answer those questions? If not, we encourage you to stop and do it again. (We only say this because we know when we're confronted like this in a book, it makes us stop to consider the action steps again.)

Now that you're back with us, how do you feel?

If we had to guess, we'd say you're feeling more determined than ever to implement the marketing plan you've drafted. That's good!

The implementation of this will be difficult, but by solidifying your foundation, you'll be able to move forward when the going gets tough.

We're going to shift gears here for a second and tell you a little bit about the house that I'm (Chase) building. I swear, we will come back around to marketing plan implementation.

When I bought the lot, I had a timeline in mind to get the house built and move our family into our dream home. That timeline is no longer even on the table. As a matter of fact, I had this wonderful text message exchange with my builder just the other day:

ME: How far behind are we?

BUILDER: We really can't say that we are ahead or behind until we get the permit. I can't do a schedule projection until then, *so really, we are just at the starting line and the race starts when we have the permit in hand.*

Two observations:

1. Get a builder who can talk in race metaphors. It softens the blow.

2. For someone who likes to go as fast as I can, hearing that we haven't even started yet—when I've already bought a lot, cleared it, and drafted plans—was the absolute worst news ever in the history of time.

Similarly, as you're implementing your marketing plan, you're going to run into obstacles that you didn't consider before. Your job as the implementer, is to do something that we've mentioned before:

Figure out the "figure-out-able." (Spoiler alert: almost everything is figure-out-able.)

What does this mean practically?

If you find yourself stuck in implementation, consider the deadline that you set in the SMART goal, and find the resources that you need to get the project done in the allotted time.

This could mean:

1. Hiring help – Maybe you don't have the time you thought you would have to do the research on social media influencers who have expressed interest in the genre you're selling your book in. Hire someone who can do that research for you. Some great platforms to consider in doing that:

   a. Upwork

   b. Fiverr

2. Look up best practices online – We live in an age where everyone wants to share their cool tactics and tricks. Use this to your advantage. The problem you're running into is likely no different than something else that someone else has overcome. So, read online about the best ways to accomplish what you're trying to do.

3. Take a break – One of the best pieces of advice we've ever heard on deadlines is to schedule procrastination into them (from Jerry Jenkins who knows a thing or two about hitting deadlines, as he's done for over 200 books that he's written). So, take a break and work on something else. Maybe that break will lead to a breakthrough on the project that you're stuck on.

4. Hire a coach or mentor – Need something more hands-on? Hire a coach or mentor to help you implement the plan. Recently, we had a consulting client who had a wonderful idea, and they had wonderful content to back it up. They got stuck in the delivery method for the content. So, they came to us, and in a couple of months, they made more progress on reaching people with that transformational content than they had made in the previous two years. Hiring a coach can get you moving faster and farther than you ever thought possible.

5. Move your deadlines – Yes, we know that deadlines are sacred, and there's a reason this is the last piece of advice. But sometimes, life gets in the way. Maybe, like me (Chase), you had a surgery, and so the book that you needed to write for the college course you were preparing needed to be pushed back a bit so that you could get it done right, instead of just getting it done. (That sounds like too personal of an example … maybe your situation is slightly different.) If that's the case, move the deadline. Implementing a bad plan because of an arbitrary deadline is worse than implementing a good plan a month or two later.

We want to talk to point 5 a bit more, because it seems completely different than everything we've said to this point. Let us be clear: Having an implementable plan full of SMART goals is the goal. Then, the goal is to run the play. But sometimes, factors outside of your control prevent you from being able to run the play—that's OK.

This is your career we're talking about, and you only have one chance to make a first impression on your readers, the influencers you're reaching out to, the publishers and agents and so forth. Take time if you need to to get things right—just don't let a pursuit of perfection keep you from forward momentum.

Let us give you a couple of examples before we move forward:

When we were getting The Nonfiction Blueprint (Jerry Jenkins' front to finish program for how to write a nonfiction book) ready for launch, the content was coming along more slowly than we had hoped. So, instead of forcing a half-baked course to maintain an arbitrary launch schedule, we were forced to push the deadline of the course back.

The result? A six-figure initial launch, and a product that will drive six figures in revenue per year for Jerry's brand for the foreseeable future. Why? Not because we launched on time, but because we launched when we knew the product was ready for consumption.

The lesson? Hold your marketing initiatives tightly—they probably don't need to change. Hold the "when" of your marketing initiatives loosely. They may need to change.

Here's a counterexample:

We mentioned earlier our work with Drs. Les and Leslie Parrott. The project we helped them with was the launch of a book called *Healthy Me, Healthy Us*. The launch date of that book happened to be May 5, 2020. If you're looking for an example of when it might have been a good idea to hold a book launch—this was it.

May 5, 2020 was right at the beginning of the COVID-19 pandemic. Amazon was experiencing shipping delays. People were nervous about the effects of the pandemic on their day-to-day lives. Most people weren't in a place to read any book, let alone self-aware enough to seek out one that helped them confront how they were feeling.

Fast-forward six month—everyone had been in isolation, some with their significant others. Their lives had been upended and people needed to know how to interact with themselves and with those they loved. Do you think that would have been a better time to launch this book?

We think so! Of course, hindsight is 20/20, but sometimes by simply pushing deadlines that we had in place, we're able to make better and more informed decisions in pushing out transformational content to those who are eagerly searching for it.

PART V

Scaling a Platform

One of the reasons that Leverage exists as a company is because authors who have had success in a first book or first book series are then starting to look at the NEXT to their platform. How do you take the inklings of success and turn them into a rich volume of future successes?

Put another way: How do you maintain momentum when you have accomplished the extremely difficult task of getting the gears moving from zero?

We call this scaling a platform, and it's difficult for different reasons than getting your book launched is difficult.

Scaling a platform requires mindset changes—shifts in the way you think—so that you can start moving from an author who has worked alone to a team leader who coordinates with experts to help take your book to the next level.

We've seen this successfully accomplished many times …

(and heck, Nashville area, where we live is full of these folks:

Donald Miller and Storybrand

Michael Hyatt and Full Focus

Dave Ramsey and his Companies

And the list goes on and on …)

… and your name could join this list! You just have to be willing to continue the journey.

So, the next several chapters are about investing in yourself. Shifting your mindset and becoming a team leader that maintains your platform's growth with ongoing strategies to take you from where you are to where you want to be.

CHAPTER 19:

Fishing Where the Fish Are

We've already talked about the origins of this lesson back in Chapter 16.

Remember the story? Ramit Sethi's dad took him and his siblings fishing at a fish hatchery, and they went to where the hatchery was releasing fish into the pond to catch fish. They caught a bunch of fish in thirty seconds. Fishing for Ramit was easy!

It reminds me of another fishing story. When I (Chase) was young, my grandfather would take me and my sister fishing at the retirement community where he lived. They had a stocked pond with perch, and there was nothing more thrilling than seeing your bob dive into the water and then catching a fish on those old timey cane rods.

What I didn't know until I was older was that my grandfather would prepare for my family to come. Early in the morning, he'd set out fishing lines, and catch the fish. Then when we got down there a little later, immediately, we'd have a fish sitting on the line for us. Fishing, for me, was easy!

If you've heard the old saying, "give a man a fish, feed him for a day, but teach a man to fish, and you feed him for a lifetime," then hopefully, you can see why I've juxtaposed these two stories.

Because of the help my grandfather gave me, I never had to find the spots in the lake where the fish were. Unlike me, Ramit's father showed him where the fish were. It's kind of like in that show *River Monsters* where the host convinces all the local fishermen to show him the spots where he can find the biggest fish. They are showing him how to fish in their particular location and situation.

You may be thinking, "Why are we still talking about fish?"

Here's the teaching point:

I can tell you where to go to find the target audience for your niche and for your brand, but that'd be like my grandfather catching the fish for me. It's fine for now, but it won't help you in the future. Instead, it's much more valuable for you to find those spots yourself.

There will be some places where you leave in the proverbial pole for weeks on end, and you don't achieve your desired results. That's OK—you simply haven't found where the fish are for your target audience.

You must keep looking until you find where your target audience hangs out online. Then, you have to keep evaluating how your message, your book, and your lead magnets are resonating with the target audience in the spot where you found them. Because the fishing spot that gets you started may not be the fishing spot that leads to scale.

For example, when we started working with Jerry, we invested heavily into content creation for his blog. We wanted him to be at or near the top of the Google search results when you search keyword phrases like "How to Write a Book." And, for the past several years, he has been!

But as we continued to grow, more and more "fishermen" (read competitors) have found that fishing spot alongside us. And that's OK!

We will always catch some fish there. But now, we need to look for additional spots to fish.

That led us to starting a YouTube Channel for Jerry, and now his videos have millions of views, and he has over 130,000 subscribers.

Why? Because at scale, one fishing hole is not going to be enough. You have to keep looking and keep searching for the next spot that your target audience will hang out at.

That's why we are so adamant about the next chapter—the testing mindset.

If you *ever* think you've arrived, you're wrong. You have to keep innovating, iterating and trying new things to stay at the top of your industry.

Keep looking for new fishing holes!

CHAPTER 20:

Testing Mindset

Do you remember the scientific method from school?

If not, here's a brief refresher:

In a typical application of <u>the scientific method</u>, a researcher (1) develops a hypothesis, (2) tests it through various means, and (3) then modifies the hypothesis on the basis of the outcome of the tests and experiments. The modified hypothesis is then (4) retested, (5) further modified, and (6) tested again, until it becomes consistent with observed phenomena and testing outcomes.

As an author, we'd encourage you to take this definition and memorize it. This is something that you're going to want to use all the days of your life.

Brainstorm > Test > Iterate > Test > Iterate

I'll give you an example of how we do this at Leverage, and then, I'll give you a few ways to walk it out in your own platform scaling efforts.

Recently, we were looking at the first time we ever did a brainstorm for Jerry. All of the ideas that we had come up with during that time had been tried. Many of them have huge levels of success. When we discovered this, we went right to our weekly meeting called The Brandstorm.

We know it's a kitschy name, but it's one of our favorite meetings of the week. In this meeting, we regularly think through a bunch of ways to grow the brands that we represent in service of our mission to help them reach as many people as possible online.

These "brandstorms" lead to some wonderful ideas. These ideas are the basis of our testing mindset at Leverage. We treat these ideas as hypotheses in that scientific method process, and we then set out to prove what we believe to be true.

And in this particular meeting, we needed to find new ideas for Jerry.

We talked through them in the first brandstorm. Then, in the next one, we developed some actionable tests for the most viable of the ideas. Over the next six months, we will run the tests, and then, we will see which ones we need to iterate on further.

By applying the scientific method to these ideas, we are staying true to who we are at Leverage, which is outlined in our second Core Value – Always Be Learning:

It's quoted in relevant part here:

2. Always Be Learning

As part of our commitment to be a great place to be and a great place to be from, we want to invest in your professional growth. We want to lay out clear paths of growth within Leverage, and we want you to grow beyond anything either of us can imagine.

So, we make learning a core piece of what we do here at Leverage. We make allowance for it both in time and in resources.

The learning resources mentioned here often come in the form of these tests.

In a client pitch meeting the other day, the brand with whom we had had tremendous success in our initial engagement said something really interesting about us. He said, "You know, if I were going to tell someone about you guys (please do…), I would certainly tell them that you do what you say you're going to do, but I don't know if I would call you digital marketing experts."

He's right. We wouldn't call ourselves digital marketing experts either.

An expert, to me, carries a connotation of arrival, of knowing everything there is to know about a particular field. At Leverage, we can't afford to be experts at social media or content marketing or conversion. Those fields are constantly changing. We can pursue excellence, but we know it will never be achieved.

Instead, the only things we want to be experts at Leverage are:

1. Running and Evaluating Tests

2. Figuring out the figure-out-able

We'll give you one more example and then, we promise, we'll apply it to you:

In January of 2021, Leverage was in peak demand. We had clients banging down our door to work with us, and we decided to run a test. We took on all the brands.

In that year, in the first six months, we launched ten products on eight different brands. Each launch had varying levels of success.

But, the learnings that we received from running the tests were incredibly valuable.

Learning #1: We can't take that many brands on at once

So, now at Leverage, we have a cadence of taking on only a few clients per year. We want to make sure that we have the time and energy to devote the appropriate amount of time to each of our brands.

Learning #2: Launch SOPs

From these launches, we developed standard operating procedures that were completely necessary to make a launch run smoothly. We use those today, and now, our launches aren't something that we fear, but something that we look forward to.

Learning #3: Brand Markers

Maybe most importantly, we started to identify the key elements that we need in the brands we work with. Things like: brands need to be able to distill their expertise to one sentence, and brands need to want to be successful more than we want the brands to be successful.

These three core learnings would not have happened without a testing mindset. If we hadn't said yes to the test, we would've taken years to formulate the three things we learned in six months' time.

So, how does this apply to your book? How does it apply to your platform?

In order to scale, you have to keep trying new things. You can't be content to only have one thing working at one time. Instead, once you identify something that is working, iterate on it to optimize or improve it. Then, when you're comfortable with how its performing, move on to the next test.

One important note: This doesn't mean that you abandon successful tests, by the way. From running that gauntlet of 8 brands, we identified two that we would continue to work with (only after a few more tests, of course). Those brands are the cornerstone of what we're building now.

Keep the things that are working, but don't forget to keep adding tests along the way.

Practically, the way we do this is to make sure that we are always running *one test per*.

You may ask what "per" means. It means one test per:

- Launch
- Brand
- Process
- Meeting

Instill a culture of running tests, and you'll constantly find ways to improve.

Building a brand is not about the destination. It's about the journey. You will never arrive, but you can always learn and grow.

CHAPTER 21:

Staying Focused

Stick with us here. You've heard countless times about the importance of staying focused and you've probably even coached someone else in your life about the same topic. But there seems to be a disconnect in many author's minds about why focus really matters in terms of marketing yourself, your books, and your content.

For most authors and creatives, focus is tough. For some, it's nearly impossible. Many people who write books are highly creative with lots of ideas and energy to pursue each of those ideas initially. Creatives often struggle with focus. Remember the Squirrel Syndrome from Part 1? If you are one of the few who doesn't struggle in this area, count yourself lucky.

For everyone else, this is another reminder that you are not alone. And you are capable of doing something about it. Focus is hard but necessary.

But some of the richest rewards come out of the discipline of focus.

I (David) have been working with authors, speakers, and online brands for nearly 20 years now. From 2005-2010, I was a booking agent for a speakers bureau. I had the privilege of working with some of the biggest names in the industry at the time—from sports, to politics, to news media, to former CEOs of major companies, and on and on. It was a wonderful season for me and it helped build the foundation I have today for working with more thought leaders.

As an agent, I was tasked with booking keynote speakers for corporate conferences and other events, and making sure each host organization was getting the best speaker possible for their audience.

At that time, the bureau I worked for was hearing from dozens of aspiring speakers every week. These were people who wanted us to represent them to our clients and to start marketing them as speakers to our large database of event planners around the world.

I quickly became inundated with requests from speakers who wanted me to pitch them to my clients. Each request would include something about how great that speaker was, why I would be foolish to not be working with them, and how my clients would benefit from their speaking ability.

I had to learn several things in this process but the most important lesson for me in those years was this: Find a way to figure out what people are great at. Everyone who came to me said they were great, so the challenge was deciding who really was vs. who wasn't.

Does this person have a unique skill set? Does that speaker have something new or different to offer? Will my clients truly benefit from paying money to bring this speaker in to talk about this topic (whatever topic the clients were facing at that time)?

I started to notice a pattern that still holds true in mind today. A lot of people came to me and said something along the lines of: "I can speak to any audience. Just put me on stage and I'll prove how good I am." It was that old idea of *just give me a chance and then I'll show you.*

At first, that sounded like a great statement. But the more I heard it and the more I dug into why people were saying it, I started to realize it was a huge red flag to watch out for. Why's that?

Focus.

Well, *lack* of focus actually.

Someone who came to me saying "just give me a chance" was actually saying, "I can do anything."

I appreciated the confidence those people had in themselves, but when you really think about how big that statement is, you start to realize it's impossible. And it was actually counterproductive to someone's career to say something like that. People who are looking to book a keynote speaker for their event typically are looking for an expert. They want someone who can come in and speak specifically about the topic or situation that matters most to them for that event. Those people didn't call me and say, "Can I please book a speaker who can do anything?"

No. They said something like: "I need a speaker to help us deal with economic uncertainty." Or, "Do you have anyone who specializes in leadership transitions and how that affects employees at all levels?" Or, "My organization is realizing we need a better approach to team building. What speakers do you have who can give us a plan in that area?"

So the speakers who came to me saying, "I can do anything" were actually telling me, "I'm not focused enough to tell you what I'm great at doing."

That is a big fat "OUCH" for some of you, right? Does that statement hit you hard? If so, better for you to recognize it now and do something to address it than for you to continue falsely presenting your brand to others and more importantly, to yourself.

So how does this apply to you as an author trying to market your book? Well, there are actually applications but the three we believe to be most important are:

1. <u>Do you have focus for what you are doing as an author and a brand?</u>

Have you decided in your own mind and heart what you are great at doing? What unique voice or perspective do you bring to your genre that will get the attention of others? I strongly suggest you take time to write a list of these things if you haven't already. Being clear in your own mind as to what you offer will greatly help you as you write, as you create your online content, as you market your manuscript, and so on. If you are overwhelmed by this idea, start your list with by writing down these simple facts:

      a. I am an author

      b. I write in the _____ genre

      c. I wrote this book because _____

      d. People who enjoy my book are likely to also enjoy books by _____(name three other authors in your genre)

      e. I'm unique in my genre because _____

      f. The reader most likely to enjoy my manuscript is ____(describe this person in as much detail as possible: age, stage of life, educational background, hobbies, family status, location of the world, etc.)

      g. As an author, I am focused on delivering _____ to my readers

2. <u>Are you able to clearly and quickly describe your focus to someone else?</u>

We've all heard of an elevator pitch before, right? It's that old scenario where you are on an elevator and you encounter someone of influence who doesn't know you, and you have the length of the elevator ride to pitch or sell or convince that person about yourself. For our purposes, let's assume you have a sixty story building to work with. If you had that elevator ride to pitch an agent or publisher, could you do it?

This takes real time and effort—it takes focus! But just because the word "focus" is something you've heard about endlessly to this point doesn't mean it's not important. It *is* important.

You'll benefit greatly from having an elevator pitch ready and being able to describe your focus quickly. If you've created the list from #1, you've got the info you need to create your elevator pitch. Now it's time to write it down and then practice saying it. This might sound like a junior high assignment, but if you are willing to put in the time and effort, it will help your career greatly. Not only will you be able to clearly articulate your brand to influential people in the industry, but more importantly, you'll be armed with that information in your own mind. You'll know exactly who you are, what you do, what you offer, why you are doing it, who you are doing it for … knowing these things are essential to focus. If you don't know this information, focus will be impossible.

Focus requires guardrails on our thinking. Creative people are cringing at that sentence right now, right? But push through the cringe! There is a time to be creative and to remove the guardrails (when you are writing your book, dreaming about your next project, making goals, brainstorming, etc.), but when it comes to describing your brand and your book, you must have guardrails. You must have focus.

So we challenge you to come up with your elevator pitch. Not just for the next agent or publisher, but for YOU. Decide who you are. Write it down. Memorize it. Say it out loud to yourself. Be willing to do a seemingly silly exercise like this in order to get clear in your own mind (and in future conversations) as to who you are as an author.

3. Choosing to have focus today doesn't mean you can't change or expand that focus in the future.

The biggest pushback we still get to this day from authors and online brands is something like: "But I am capable of doing many different things. Why do I need to just focus on one?"

Of course you are capable of doing many different things. We all are. But you are NOT capable of doing all of those many different things simultaneously. And even if you somehow (unlikely) are able to do many different things all at once, you are not able to do them all at a high level. It's just not possible. Your ability to multitask is not an excuse to ignore focus. Most people give way too much credit to their multitasking skills and not nearly enough credit to the power of focus. Don't be most people.

Pick a priority and focus.

Notice we said "priority" there? We did not say pick your priorities. Did you know the original version of the word "priority" never had a plural tense attached?

We learned this when reading a stellar book by Greg McKeown called *Essentialism*. That book and really anything created by Greg is worth your time, but for now, let's focus on the word "priority." See what we did there?

The root word never had a plural version. In fact, the original word existed in singular tense only for over 500 years. That is before (probably us Americans) figured out a way to screw it up. We decided to discard 500 years of meaning and instead turn this word into something new, just for us.

Somehow, modern English speakers took a beautiful, wonderful, meaningful word like "priority" and added a plural tense to it and ruined it. And in doing so, not only has the word been tarnished, but many people are struggling to keep up with priority lists and they can't figure out why.

Does that sound familiar to you, too? If so, the reason you've struggled in this area and the reason you haven't featured it out is this:

There should not be any such thing as a priority list. There should be a priority. That's it. No list.

You can tell I (David) am a little irritated about this topic, right? The reason I'm upset is because for most of my adult life, I lived under the false assumption that I needed to have all of my priorities lined up and that I should be making progress on each one simultaneously.

It's not true. Relieve yourself of that false thinking right now.

So rather than choosing to do many different things at a low or mediocre level, try doing one thing at a high level—one thing as your focus for now. Choose your priority. Then as you have more information and more opportunities, reevaluate and decide if your focus should stay the same or if it should change.

Just because you choose to focus your brand and your books and your content in a specific place today doesn't mean you can't change or expand in the future. But it is much easier to choose a focus, establish yourself in that area of focus, then expand to other areas of focus, than it is to attempt to tackle everything at once and just hope that something catches.

If you choose to tackle everything and just hope something takes off, you are essentially playing the lottery. Is playing the lottery bad? Not necessarily. Is it a wise financial investment? No.

The preferred alternative is to invest intentionally over time, and adjust your approach as needed along the way. Take the bold step to deduce what your focus is and run with it. See what happens. Be willing to fail and be ready to adjust. But don't get distracted by the temptation to do more or different than what you've established as your focus.

Changing an area of focus is not a bad thing; not choosing an area of focus is almost always a bad thing.

4. BONUS APPLICATION - for authors who are specifically trying to build an audience online!

From the example we described about keynote speakers earlier, the last application to be highlighted in this section is for those of you who are intentionally working on building your following online. This could be through social media platforms, podcasts, YouTube, email lists, or any other form of audience gathering.

The idea of focus applies to building an audience also. There are so many different places you could be spending your time to build an audience, so it is imperative to create your plan for how you will spend your time. You are an author, so we assume you are more interested in writing your next book or blog post than you are creating your online marketing strategy, right?

And if you haven't yet reached commercial success with your book, you are likely supplementing your efforts with a job. Plus, you have family, friends, and other obligations. There are many plates spinning in your life, so you must be focused when it comes to the time and efforts you are putting forth online.

Start with the low hanging fruit. Are you currently active on any social media platforms or in any genre-specific forums? If there are places you are currently engaging online, use that as your initial test.

Warning — we used the word "initial" intentionally. Online audience building is a complicated puzzle and there is no roadmap for everyone to follow. Each author, each audience, each situation is different. Authors must go into the online audience building game with the mindset of test - iterate - test - iterate. Revisit chapter 19 for more on this approach.

Be willing to commit ninety days at a time to your social media tests. From a marketing standpoint, there isn't anything that can happen in one day that will determine if you should stay or leave a certain social media platform. You have to give it time, whatever "it" happens to be for you.

Decide to spend the next ninety days on the platform you enjoy the most. Create a blueprint for what you are going to do. If you don't know how to create a blueprint, start with:

- The content you will create

- The frequency you will post

- How much you will interact with others

- The numbers that will decide if you should continue or iterate

Measure where you are when you start the ninety days and then reassess where you are after the ninety days are over. Did your followers or likes grow? Did your engagement increase? Are you still enjoying the process or has it become miserable for you? This is another example of authors needing to take off the creative hat and put on the analytical hat for a minute. If it's working, figure out your next plan. Iterate and come up with how you'll approach the next ninety days. If your original test isn't working, GREAT! Now you know what not to do. So come up with your next ninety day text on a different platform. Repeat this process until you find where your content, your personality, your expertise, and your audience all converge.

If you are willing to devote a set amount of time to testing these platforms, you'll start to gather the data necessary to make your next decision.

Guessing is great when you are coming up with your tests. But after that, let the data guide your next decisions.

**An additional note for those of us who try to focus (really, we do), but find it difficult.

I (Chase) intentionally asked David to take the lead on this chapter because I'm not the one to preach about focus. But one key takeaway for me from the book *Imagine It Forward* by Beth Comstock was to divide your time into buckets:

70 percent for Core Projects (to be accomplished in the next twelve months)

20 percent for Next Projects (to be accomplished in the next two to three years)

10 percent for Inflection Projects (to be accomplished in the next five to seven years)

Having a framework to allow myself to dream big has helped me to maintain focus in the core activities that run our business. You might find the above framework helpful. If not, continue to search out ways you can build focus intentionally into your day-to-day.

CHAPTER 22:

Building Your Team

As we've discussed already, you as an author are most likely a creative mind. You are outstanding at your specific area of expertise. You are a talented and genuine voice when it comes to the craft of writing.

But you might not be bringing other essential skill sets to the table when it comes to building your brand.

That is OK.

I (David) worked with an author for a long time who was (and still is) one of the smartest people I've ever been around. His memory was nearly flawless. Because he could remember almost every conversation he'd ever had or book he'd ever read, his ability to recall that information and integrate it into a current situation was astounding.

On top of that, his gift of the ability to tell a story was unmatched. I realize I'm biased when saying this, but this guy was a master at the craft of storytelling. He could rope you in with an initial statement that both intrigued you and confused you, then he'd start talking about something else that had zero connection to the first statement. Then through humor and intentional pauses and crafty phrasing, he'd eventually bring the story to culmination and connect all the dots. Multiple times, at the end of those stories I found my mouth hanging open in astonishment at the roller coaster of emotions someone had just taken me on … through spoken words. It was raw, God-given talent that had been honed and crafted and expertly manipulated over the years. Astonishing.

That same author, a mentor and hero of mine, would be the first to tell you that as great as he is at storytelling, he's equally bad at several other things. His wife would be the first to nod and agree with that statement.

The point is that as his career as an author and a speaker began to take off, it became obvious he needed to build a team around him to help in the areas where he wasn't gifted.

For many authors who are starting out in the marketing journey for their books, the idea of building a team isn't applicable today. But even if you aren't able to build a team around you right now, it is still a good exercise to be thinking about the areas you might need help in the future.

Building a team, especially for an author, is a challenge because it requires you to be willing to let go of certain things and trust someone else to be your representative in those areas. Authors usually struggle to let go of creative control. When it comes to the content of a book or blog post or email, an author should be highly cautious about letting go of that creative control because the author is the expert. That's the unique voice you are bringing to the table, so it makes sense you'd be reluctant to let someone else who is not an expert be allowed to make the decisions in that area.

But just like you are the expert in your content, someone else might be the expert when it comes to the positioning strategy of your content in the marketplace. You are the expert and authority in your subject matter or in your story. Someone else is likely the expert in your website copy, your email strategy, your social posting frequency, your overall brand business approach, and so on.

You are doing all of these things on your own early in your career, but you will not be doing all of these things on your own as your career progresses and as your brand continues to grow. So where do you start when it comes to building a team?

Consider these questions first:

- Outside of writing my book(s), are there any other areas of this brand creation and audience building process that I am uniquely qualified for? (e.g. interpersonal communication, blog post or email creation, social media post creation and implementation, making the brand financially viable through book sales and/or creation of other ancillary products)

- Are there any areas I am eager to *not* be involved with in the future? (e.g. website creation, SEO, social media strategy and implementation, email list sequences, accounting, sales copy, managing incoming communications, customer service)

- What would need to be happening (financial returns, social media engagement, brand awareness) in order for me to bring on someone else to help in these efforts?

Come up with a list, in order of importance, of what you would want as part of your team. Decide what positions and tasks you will need help with and then start watching for people who might fit those roles.

At Leverage, we put this concept into practice by asking our team to annually create a Love & Loathe list. This is exactly what it sounds like—a list of things each team member loves doing as part of their responsibilities at our company, and then a list of things they loathe doing. The Loathe list can also include things someone simply isn't good at doing. We've had many situations where someone on our staff raised their hand and said "I'm happy to keep trying this thing, but just so you know, I'm not very good at it." Things like that are fine to add to the Loathe list.

And we always remind each person that we can't guarantee we will remove every item on someone's Loathe list, but it helps for all of us to be aware of the things that someone doesn't enjoy doing. We are a business, so work needs to be done by someone, but if we know what each person is excited about doing and which things they dread, that helps us build towards making improvements whenever possible.

The same applies to you as an author. Your Love list might be a lot shorter than your Loathe list, but because you are on the journey by yourself for now, you have to do everything regardless of whether you like it or not. Just making the Loathe list and starting to think about the things you would like to pass off at some point will help you mentally today, and also with implementation in the future.

Once you have a Loathe list to work from and once you are ready to start adding others around you to help in the efforts you'll most likely need to start with people you know. Someone who is a friend or someone at your church or a young person you know who is looking to gain experience. All of those options are on the table when a brand is still in its early stages. For those people, it will be essential for you to have your focus and your elevator pitch (see Chapter 21) down because you must clearly convey to them what you are doing and why. People will latch on to vision if they trust you and if they believe in the plan you are putting in front of them to execute (see Chapter 23).

Figure out a way to clearly communicate the purpose of what you are doing with your brand, your content, your book. Do that well and people will be eager to join you in the journey.

There are a variety of wonderful resources on team building practically, so we don't need to spend too much more time on it here, but a couple of crucial reads that I'd suggest to look into on the topic are:

What Got You Here Won't Get You There by Marshall Goldsmith

Radical Candor by Kim Scott

It's Your Ship by Michael Abrashoff

CHAPTER 23:

Minding the Vision Gap with Your Team

I (Chase) always admired the phrase that the British use on the Underground, "Mind the gap." The phrase is such a polite way to encourage people not to plunge to their death underneath the voltage and tonnage of an underground train.

Similarly, a gap in vision between you and your team can have fatal consequences to your budding author brand. So, you must mind that gap. Let me explain with an example.

100 million people per year will interact with Leverage's content.

That's what I told David when we were trying to home in on what our vision would be. Of course, knowing me, that meant that we were trying to capture the vision the day before we were supposed to communicate the vision to the team.

David is one of the rare ones who usually understands what I mean when I say dumb and crazy things like that. And so, in that moment, he made me stop from the fantastical and bring it to a team level of interaction.

I believe his exact words were something like:

"That's great, Chase, but what does it mean for our team today? Reaching 100 million people per year is a crazy goal. People will roll their eyes and dismiss the idea if we don't take the time to be intentional about the way we present our vision and how we plan to get there."

As we started to talk through it together, David and I realized that what I was trying to say is that by 2038, Leverage will work with 100 brands, each of which reach one million people per year with transformational content.

As of this writing, we are on track to reach 2.7 million people in year two of this audacious vision (which puts us right on track).

But do you see how the big picture statement at the top of this chapter provided no real direction for our team? Can you see how the more specific vision seems more real? More achievable?

In the same way, as you build your team, your job will be to hold the big picture vision. But the gap between vision and action is where your leadership will shine.

After that conversation, David and I realized that a sixteen-year vision was great, but that we also needed a shorter term vision for our team to shoot for. So, as we are looking at what we need to accomplish in the next sixteen years, we broke it down farther, and at our last quarterly summit, we introduced our Vision 2030.

You have to make sure that you make your vision actionable by minding that vision gap!

There are several ways to do this:

1. Get a David—but you can't have our David

2. Work through your vision by thinking how each of your team members will respond to it

3. Cultivate team buy-in

Let's talk about the last two a bit more:

When you work through your vision by thinking how each of your team members will respond to it, you accomplish several things. First, you start to see how different personalities might react to an audacious vision. Think for instance, about how your accountant will laugh when you tell them your dreams. Why is that? It's because their job is to look at what is, not what will be. So, when you try to move their horizon from the page in front of them to the vision of the future, you have to meet them where they are.

Second, by looking at the vision through each team members' lens, you develop empathy with them.

I'll be honest with you: Empathy is not my strong suit. As a matter of fact, it may be my weak suit, along with caring too much and working too hard (*The Office* reference for those of you still with me).

So, by forcing myself to empathize with my team members, I get to see the role that they can play in the ultimate vision, and I can start to coach them to see in themselves what I see in them.

And when you start to coach them, you'll find that you're able to cultivate team buy-in.

That buy-in is critical.

I remember early on at Leverage, we had a team of contractors who were incredibly gifted at what they did. They knew the business, and they knew how to maximize what we were doing. So, we brought them in for our very first quarterly summit. In that summit, we set a goal based on revenue generation. The goal was to hit $500,000 in revenue in a certain amount of time. I even had a graph that included a stick figure in an unfilled tank. We were going to try to drown that character I'd created in cash—the cash generated during the timeline we'd set at the summit. The character's name was Half-a-Mil Milly.

Spoiler: We didn't drown Milly.

Why? Not because we didn't have a plan and not because the goal was crazy. Instead, it was because as one contractor put it: "We're contractors. You're not paying us for results, you're paying us to complete the work being assigned. We want you to succeed, but why would we care specifically about your revenue generation goals?"

And you know what? He was right. The question hit us hard and it hurt at first, but the more we thought about it, the more we agreed that he was right.

We, as leaders of teams, need to understand that we can't force people to care as much as we do. But we can cultivate buy-in by giving them a clear picture of what they could do as part of our team. When we do that, we get the greatest management gift of all—the gift of not delegation, but multiplication.

One final example from what we've learned while running Leverage.

Our company started in 2018 and within that first year, Chase and I (David) settled on what we believed should be our core values. Chapter 18 of this book talked in depth about what our fourth core value is today, but that specific value was only added to our company earlier this year (2022).

Our original fourth core value was "A want-to, not have-to mindset"

Our intention when creating that original version was, in part, a response to the Half-a-Mil Milly situation. We heard our contractors say they didn't care about the same things that we did as founders, so we set out to create a core value that emphasized our desire for Leverage team members to truly want to be doing the work we gave them each day. Instead of being a place where they had to perform tasks in order to receive payment, we were hoping to instill a value that encouraged people to enjoy their work—to want to do it rather than to have to do it.

That core value stayed in place at our company for several years but after much thought, prayer, and discussion, it became clear to me and Chase that we were missing the mark.

The core values of a company should be the non-negotiable elements that everyone agrees are essential. It would be wonderful if everyone truly wanted to do every part of their job every single day, but that's not realistic. The truth is that we all have certain things we do as a part of our job that just have to be done even if we don't want to do them.

So we updated our fourth core value (again, see Chapter 18 for the details on what we chose to replace the old version with); and instead of requiring our team to "want to" do our work, we removed that core value from our list. Now, our challenge has become to cultivate more buy-in from each person who works with us. We strive to share our vision and our dream for Leverage, and to use our passion for what we do to draw others in to join our mission.

We paint the picture for what we are doing collectively and we map out what each person's role could look like in those efforts. We show them what we do and we dream with them about what we could all be doing together in the future, and that is proving helpful already and resulting in noticeable multiplication.

To scale your platform, you're going to need as much multiplication as you can get.

PART VI

You've Got This

You have the necessary tools now to plan and execute an amazing book launch. You have what you need to start scaling your platform after your launch, and so in these last two chapters, we simply want to offer you some words of encouragement.

We've been lucky enough in our careers to work with some of the most established and successful creative professionals that you can imagine. We've rubbed shoulders with folks that other people dream of meeting.

Guess what? They are people just like you.

There's no magic potion they took to get to where they are. They just didn't stop working when it would have been so easy to.

Take these last two chapters as our charge to you. You can do this.

And if you ever need help, feel free to reach out to us. We'd love to have a conversation with you about what you are doing and be a resource to you as you face the challenges of being an author.

CHAPTER 24:

Everyone Starts As Unknown

Sometimes, the best words to cover a certain topic have already been written by someone else, and so for this chapter we are bringing in a guest.

Here's a little encouragement for you from 21-time New York Times Bestselling Author, Jerry Jenkins:

Do You Want to Become an Author?

Because you've found this [book], I'm guessing you have a passion for writing. In fact, maybe you want to be more than a writer — you want to be an author.

Do you have a story inside you burning to be told, but something's keeping you from writing it?

Maybe:

- You're overwhelmed, having no idea how or where to start.
- You started but quickly found yourself mired in doubt, worried you're headed the wrong direction.
- You wrote your book but are now frustrated to the point of desperation by a growing pile of rejection slips.

Regardless, you've come to the right place.

I Was Once Unknown and Unpublished

If you know my work, it's probably because of *Left Behind*, my New York Times bestselling novel series. But actually I've written more than 200 books across several genres (including biographies of several famous people), and my writing has also appeared in magazines like TIME, Reader's Digest, Parade, and many others.

But it wasn't always this way. I started where most writers do—unknown and unpublished. I wrote my first several books on a manual typewriter that sat on a board suspended between two chairs, while my family was sleeping. I learned early that there are no shortcuts to publishing success.

When I was a teenager, an author I admired took an hour to advise me, and I vowed that if I ever succeeded, I'd pay forward that kindness.

I believe that with basic skills and proper guidance, you can learn to create prose that entertains, touches hearts, and has the potential to impact lives all over the world. That happened for me, a small town Midwestern kid, so why not you?

Thanks, Jerry!

Why not you?

You may feel the weight of being unknown. You may see the insurmountable tasks in front of you for marketing your book and building and scaling your platform. You may even feel the pangs of self-doubt that Jerry mentioned above.

But hey, you've made it this far in a book about author marketing, for crying out loud! You have a deep desire to write, publish, and market a book and to do it well.

And you know what? We believe that you can do it.

Do you believe that too?

CHAPTER 25:

You Can Do It

Part 1 = David

In 2010, I left the speakers bureau that I mentioned earlier in this book (Chapter 21). I left for a few a variety of reasons but the two main factors in my decision were:

1. I'd hit my ceiling at that company. The job was great. The pay was great. The people and connections and opportunities were all great. But the ceiling was obvious. I believed that I could not go any higher than the point I'd reached in 2010.

2. There was a burning desire in my soul to do something on my own. I'd worked in a giant radio market previously, then been at one of the largest speakers bureaus in the country for five years. Each of those stops was useful, but they were under the umbrella of something I could not control or even really influence. I wanted to know if I could do it … on my own.

So I left on good terms from the bureau and started my own author consulting company. I had no idea what I was really doing from a business perspective, but I was willing to move forward anyway.

I was brought on retainer by one management company immediately and over time, I was able to build a considerable business by coaching authors and speakers how to create revenue between book releases and on days/weeks when they weren't giving keynote presentations.

Over the next seven years I helped to build multiple brands, multiple products, multiple bestselling books, and multiple millions in annual revenue. I had taken something that I had no idea about and over time had turned it into a notable business venture. Mission accomplished. Things were going great. I did it!

Then it all went away, almost overnight. Not too long after deciding to devote almost all of my time to a small stable of authors, the management company representing those authors dissolved in a shocking and tragic way. In less than thirty days, the position of influence I had, the financial "guarantees" I had earned, the job security I'd built ... it was all gone.

So once again, the unknown was knocking at my door.

Answering that knock was the absolute right move for me. In doing so, Chase Neely and I partnered in a new business that has gone on to create online presences and products for brands in a variety of niches. We've created content and products that have reached around the world. We've been able to partner with groups in Europe and Asia on different projects. We've brought content from our authors and experts to multiple millions of people each year and that number continues to grow. We've been able to provide jobs to dozens of people since January 2018, and as of this writing, we have nine full-time employees, six contractors, and four interns! And the forecast for the next phase of our company is even more exciting!

This didn't happen because I'm some wizard at author marketing or platform building. It happened because I was willing to face the unknown.

It's one thing to talk about writing a book, or to feel called to write a book, or to have the desire to write a book. It's a completely different thing to actually go and write that book.

It's unknown.

Until you start. Until you learn.

It's unknown until it becomes known.

Facing the unknown is something every author goes through at some point. It's not optional. You must decide that you are willing and ready to go through things you have no idea how to handle.

This book will help you but this book is not the one-stop answer for all of your questions. You still need to decide if you are willing to face the unknown, and to keep moving forward no matter what happens.

The truth is that you are completely capable of facing the unknown. Of course you can do it. And that isn't some platitude to be put up on your wall in a frame on a nice picture with an eagle perched in some majestic setting. This is real.

The question is not *can* you do it because yes, you can. The question is, are you willing to do it?

Are you willing to do it?

Are you willing to take the time to make the lists and set the goals we've mapped out in this book? Are you willing to spend the creative energy necessary to document what you are trying to do and how you plan on accomplishing it? Are you willing to answer all the questions we've suggested you consider in this book? Are you willing to do what it takes to achieve whatever goals you've attached to this project?

Are you willing to choose a priority?

Are you willing to keep going? To be methodical, with purpose, with intention?

Are you willing to test and iterate? Then test and iterate again?

Are you willing to commit specific amounts of time to certain efforts in order to get specific amounts of information that will inform your next steps?

Are you willing to face the unknown until it becomes known?

I believe you are able to do this, to face the unknown. But what I believe doesn't really matter to you.

What do you believe?

Part 2 = Chase

11 years ago, I packed up my family and moved to Nashville, Tennessee.

I wanted to represent people from each major creative field as an entertainment attorney. I had no job, $1,500 in the bank, and a twelve-month lease on a house that cost $1,000 per month.

It was the point of no return.

I was either going to figure it out, or I was going to fail. But one way or another, I was going to find out if I had what it took to succeed.

Since then, I've represented *New York Times* bestselling authors, award-winning songwriters, a Grammy-nominated artist who appeared on *American Idol*, an actress on a major Netflix series, and even a racecar driver (for good measure).

I've reached my goal. The dream is in-hand.

But, too often, that's all creative entrepreneurs are shown. The beginning and the end.

We're shown the picture at the beginning of the seven years and then again at the end. We hear about the idea for the bestseller and see it hit the *New York Times* list. We see the child receive the violin for Christmas and then hear them as an adult in the symphony.

But, we often miss what happens in the middle.

We find ourselves asking:

What does it take to go from beginner to expert?

But, for many of us, that's the wrong question. Because we're not beginners anymore. We've grown the ability and the dream. We know we are able to do what we've set out to do.

But the question we can't answer is this:

Why, with my talent and ability, am I unable to make the switch between struggling creative and award winner?

The answer is almost too easy:

Perseverance.

When I was six months into my journey—having passed the bar exam, but still working as a glorified intern at a music publishing company—I couldn't see the light at the end of the tunnel.

But the dream carried me.

Three-and-a-half years later, when my first business struggled to break even, it was even harder to imagine the future I'm living now.

Five years in, when those who had started the journey with me began to give up, the dream was a distant thought.

I'm not where I am today because of any special skill I had.

Instead, I'm here because I refused to give up.

That business I started that was only breaking even?

I shut it down and went back to the drawing board for another idea.

My law firm that lived off of referrals?

I re-invested in systems that would continuously bring in referrals.

I'm convinced the next great American novel has been written. The next Taylor Swift is already performing. The next great businessperson is out there already working on their business.

These things are cyclical. Look through history, there's always a next superstar in every industry.

If you have the talent, and you want that person to be you, here's my advice:

Persevere.

One of my authors was rejected fifty-one times before his first publishing deal.

That book became a *New York Times* bestseller six months *after* launch, long after the publisher stopped pushing it. The author never quit.

Persevere.

Recently, a songwriter of mine realized her dream of signing with a major publishing company—hundreds of songs and *over a decade* after beginning her journey.

Persevere.

One of my artists performed a show several years ago in the first winter storm in New York City. Eighteen people showed up. Recently, one of his songs crossed 100 million streams on Spotify.

Persevere.

In this world, everyone is talented. Everyone is smart. Everyone has the innate ability to succeed.

They may just be lacking one key quality.

After reading this book, I pray that you do not. My hope for you is that you persevere.

Because the world needs your message.

The world needs your encouragement. We need to hear from people for whom life has not always been easy. We need to hear from the survivors, the misfits—those courageous enough to bare their soul without flinching.

What have you learned? What has galvanized you? How have you raised yourself up from where you started?

Recently, I was attending a dress rehearsal for our local symphony's next performance, and I couldn't help but imagine how dull our world would be if creative professionals gave up.

As I watched the synchronized bow strokes of the string sections and heard the timely thunder of the timpani, I imagined the violinist who threw her bow on the ground in disgust after a failed audition.

I imagined the guitarist who popped a D-string in the middle of a performance and walked off the stage.

I imagined the author who put the manuscript away after two well-written and edited chapters.

I imagined a world where the person we need to hear from most gave up too soon, so I urge you again:

Please, for all of our sakes, Persevere.

AFTERWORD

From David:

I'm sitting on my back porch as I type this. My wife, Stephanie, has called me in for dinner three times and I just haven't been able to stop putting the final touches on this book yet … don't worry though, she gets me! I haven't gone in yet because I can't stop thinking about how the words in these pages are just the surface of what I've learned so far about author marketing. What's even scarier is with all I know and with all Chase knows about these subjects, there is so much more we don't know. The older I get, the more I realize there is a lot I don't know—but that doesn't stop me from moving forward, from a desire to learn and to become more.

I'm honored to do the work we do and to work with the people I get to interact with every day because of Leverage Brands. The authors, the experts, the brands, the team of specialists who help us every single day in order for the company to thrive. I'm thankful for every single part of it.

My hope is that this book will be the catalyst for you to embark on your own journey. A journey you've been thinking about for a long time now. Don't let the opportunity pass you by. If even one chapter or paragraph of this book was meaningful to you, run with it! There is no perfect textbook or roadmap for authors to follow. Find whatever makes sense to you or whatever resonates with you and go!

You are the only thing standing in your way right now. Resist the temptation to blame someone else or something else for your lack of progress. Decide today that you are able, regardless of your current circumstances, to determine your next steps.

ABOUT THE AUTHORS

Chase Neely and David Loy are co-founders of Leverage Brands Co. They have a passion for helping authors, speakers, and brands who have transformational content to maximize their reach online.

Surrounded by a team of experts, Chase and David are eagerly persevering into the unknown each day.

If you want to chat about where you are as an author, and determine if Leverage Brands might be able to help you on your journey, visit LeverageBrands.co for more information.